Teaching About the Holocaust in English Secondary Schools:

An empirical study of national trends, perspectives and practice

Teaching About the Holocaust in English Secondary Schools
An empirical study of national trends, perspectives and practice

Alice Pettigrew
Stuart Foster
Jonathan Howson
Paul Salmons
Ruth-Anne Lenga
Kay Andrews

ISBN 13: 978-1-905351-11-4
ISBN 10: 1-905351-11-9

Copyright © Alice Pettigrew & Stuart Foster

Published in Great Britain in 2009
Department of Arts and Humanities
Institute of Education
University of London
20 Bedford Way
London WC1H 0AL
United Kingdom

Copy requests:
Stuart Foster
Department of Arts and Humanities
Institute of Education
University of London
20 Bedford Way
London WC1H 0AL
United Kingdom
s.foster@ioe.ac.uk

Typeset using Frutiger LT Std 57 Cn

British Library Cataloguing-in-Publication Data
A CIP record is available from the British Library

ABOUT THE HEDP

This research report has been written under the auspices of the Holocaust Education Development Programme (HEDP). The HEDP is part of the Institute of Education, University of London and comprises full and part-time researchers and educators:

- *Director*, Dr Stuart Foster
- *Head of Research and Evaluation*, Jonathan Howson
- *Head of Curriculum and Development*, Paul Salmons
- *National Outreach Co-ordinator*, Kay Andrews
- *Research and Evaluation Officer*, Dr Alice Pettigrew
- *Specialist Adviser*, Ruth-Anne Lenga
- *Programme Administrator*, Kristen Dammers
- *Research I.T. Consultant*, Dr Evangelos Himonides
- *External Consultant*, Dr Melissa Carson.

The research was developed in order to inform the design and delivery of a high quality, high impact continuing professional development (CPD) programme that has the potential to profoundly shape teaching and learning about the Holocaust by addressing critical questions for teachers.

Places on the CPD programme are available free of charge to teachers from every state secondary and middle school in England. The programme workshops are delivered regionally by world-recognised experts. For workshop participants, the CPD programme also offers distance learning through a Virtual Learning Environment which provides ongoing resources and development opportunities.

Further information about the HEDP and its CPD programme can be found at www. hedp.org.uk

CONTENTS

AUTHORS

The principal authors of this research report are: Dr Alice Pettigrew, Dr Stuart Foster, Jonathan Howson and Paul Salmons. From the initial design of a research proposal to the final preparation of this written report, the authors have been guided and informed by Ruth-Anne Lenga and Kay Andrews, both experts in the field of Holocaust Education.

ACKNOWLEDGEMENTS

We are particularly indebted to Holocaust historian Professor Yehuda Bauer for his support, critical advice and wise counsel throughout the research process.

A number of colleagues, both within the Holocaust Education Development Programme team and elsewhere within the Institute of Education have also contributed significantly to the research and writing of this report. Particular thanks are due to: Kristen Dammers and Dr Evangelos Himonides. Furthermore, Dr James Brown, Dr Melissa Carson, Professor Alex Moore, Dr Ioulia Papageorgi and Jo Pearce provided valuable support and advice.

The design and development of this research also benefited from in-depth discussions with a number of individuals and organisations already working within the field of Holocaust education. A full list of these individuals and organisations is provided in Appendices 2 and 3.

The authors would also like to thank the members of the HEDP Advisory Board including representatives from The Pears Foundation, the Department for Children, Schools and Families and the Holocaust Educational Trust for their detailed feedback on interim drafts of this report and for their recommendations and involvement in the programme since its inception in 2008.

Finally, everyone associated with the HEDP is especially grateful to all the teachers who generously gave up their time to complete the online survey and to those who shared their thoughts and experiences during school-based interviews conducted in the spring of 2009.

EXECUTIVE SUMMARY

This research was commissioned by The Pears Foundation and the Department for Children, Schools and Families (DCSF). The aims were to examine when, where, how and why the Holocaust is taught in state-maintained secondary schools in England, and to inform the design and delivery of a continuing professional development (CPD) programme for teachers who teach about the Holocaust. A two-phase mixed methodology was employed. This comprised an online survey which was completed by 2,108 respondents and follow-up interviews with 68 teachers in 24 different schools throughout England.

The research reveals that teachers adopt a diverse set of approaches to this challenging and complex subject. In the report, teachers' perceptions, perspectives and practice are presented and a range of challenges and issues encountered by teachers across the country are explicitly identified. The research shows that, although most teachers believe that it is important to teach about the Holocaust, very few have received specialist professional development in this area. It also shows that many teachers find it a difficult and complicated subject to teach, and that they both want and need support to better equip them to teach about the Holocaust effectively.

The report is the largest endeavour of its kind in the UK in both scope and scale. The authors hope it will be of considerable value to all those concerned with the advancement and understanding of Holocaust education both in the UK and internationally.

KEY FINDINGS

Where and when does teaching about the Holocaust take place?

1. Teaching about the Holocaust appears to take place in a wide variety of subject areas within English secondary schools. Among those who responded to the survey, the largest proportions of teachers who had taught about the Holocaust reported that they principally did so within history (55% of respondents, n591),[1] religious education (RE) (25%, n269), English (7%, n72), citizenship (3%, n34) and personal, social and health education (PSHE) (3%, n33).

2. Data from the survey also reveals that teaching about the Holocaust currently occurs across all seven years of compulsory and post-compulsory secondary education with a clear concentration in Year 9, the final year of Key Stage 3. It appears that it is only in Year 9 that history becomes the dominant subject area in which teaching about the Holocaust takes place. If a student encounters the Holocaust at school in Years 7 and 8, it is likely that this will take place in a subject other than history, most notably within RE.

---

[1] When completing the survey, it was possible for respondents to entirely skip any individual question. As a consequence, the total number of responses received fluctuated throughout the survey. Unless otherwise stated, the percentages presented in this report have been calculated from the total number of teachers who submitted any response to the pertinent question. All percentages are accompanied by a numeric 'n' figure: this indicates exactly how many responses are being described.

3. The research reports considerable variation in the amount of time spent teaching about the Holocaust both within and across individual subject areas, year groups and key stages. Within Key Stage 3 history, where the Holocaust is a compulsory component of the National Curriculum, some teachers reported spending one hour on the topic while others suggested they spent more than 20 hours. In Year 9 history, teachers most commonly reported spending approximately six hours teaching about the Holocaust.

Exploring teachers' aims, understandings and pedagogical practice

4. One of the most commonly reported challenges to teaching about the Holocaust was managing limited curriculum time. As a consequence, some teachers appear to find it difficult to know how to decide what content they should include.

5. Analysis of the topics that teachers report including in their teaching tentatively suggests that, rather than explore victims' responses to persecution and genocide, teachers are more likely to focus on perpetrator-oriented narratives.[2] Two content areas appear to dominate teachers' coverage of the Holocaust: the period of persecution in the 1930s and a focus on Auschwitz-Birkenau. Other key aspects of the Holocaust, including the pre-war lives of Jewish people and important stages in the development of genocide (for example, the *Einsatzgruppen*, Wannsee Conference and Operation Reinhard) appear to receive less attention.

6. 73% (n851) of teachers who completed the survey and had experience of teaching about the Holocaust indicated that they were confident and 'very knowledgeable' about the subject. However, the responses given to a series of nine 'knowledge-based' questions reveal some potentially important gaps in historical understanding. While the research shows that some teachers demonstrate very detailed specialist subject knowledge and clear understanding, it appears that for others, knowledge of the Holocaust is perhaps often drawn largely from popular rather than academic discourse.

7. When asked to consider what the term, 'the Holocaust' means, the most commonly shared understanding among teachers is that the Holocaust was the persecution and murder of a range of victims targeted by the Nazi regime. This was true irrespective of a teacher's prior experience of teaching about the Holocaust or their subject background. Of note, however, the teachers who appeared most knowledgeable about the history of the Holocaust (as determined by responses given to the knowledge-based questions included in the survey) were also those most likely to use the term to mean the specific targeting of European Jews.

8. 85.1% (n887) of those who completed the survey and who had experience of teaching in this area believe that it is right that the Holocaust is a compulsory part of the secondary school history curriculum. However, many teachers found it difficult to articulate the distinct historical significance of the Holocaust. More regularly, the Holocaust was framed by teachers in terms of 'universal lessons,' often divorced from any specific historical

---

[2] Such narratives focus on the actions of Nazi soldiers and the Nazi government and position Jewish people as objects rather than subjects of study.

context. Irrespective of subject background, in both the survey and follow-up interviews, teachers were more likely to describe their practice when approaching the Holocaust in terms of broad, overarching objectives such as tackling racism or encouraging respect for diversity than to do so with reference to distinct, subject-specific teaching aims. Making a study of the Holocaust 'relevant' in the context of twenty-first century classrooms, appeared, for many teachers, to be a key concern.

Supporting teachers in Holocaust education

9. 94.7% (n1,002) of all teachers who responded to the survey and who had experience in this area considered that it would always be important to teach about the Holocaust. However, 41.3% (n426) said that they believed it was difficult to do so effectively. In addition to the challenge of organising content within limited curriculum time, other reported difficulties include: managing effective cross-curricular co-operation, dealing with emotional content and responding to some students' misunderstandings and prejudice.

10. During interview, a number of teachers acknowledged the importance of support from a variety of specialist Holocaust education organisations working in England. However, data from the survey suggests that, at a national level, many teachers remain unaware of the support that is currently available to them. The data also suggests that very few teachers who teach about the Holocaust have received any form of specialist professional development in the subject and 82.5% (n952) consider themselves self-taught. 77.5% (n765) of the teachers who took part in the survey with experience in this area indicated that they would be interested in attending a workshop for related continuing professional development.

In March 2006, the UK delegation of the Task Force for International Cooperation on Holocaust Education, Remembrance and Research (ITF) submitted a report on the provision of education about the Holocaust in UK schools. Many of the ITF's questions were considered 'impossible to answer' because there was insufficient research evidence from which to report.

The HEDP research aims to help address that gap by providing a more comprehensive empirical portrait of Holocaust education in England's secondary schools than has ever existed before.

CHAPTER 1: INTRODUCTION

BACKGROUND TO THE HOLOCAUST EDUCATION DEVELOPMENT PROGRAMME

In April 2007, The Pears Foundation – a UK based charitable foundation – and the British Government announced that they would jointly commit £1.5 million funding over a three-year period to provide professional development for teachers who teach about the Holocaust in England's secondary schools.[3] The following year, the Holocaust Education Development Programme, or HEDP, was established within the Institute of Education at the University of London.[4] The HEDP was given responsibility for developing and delivering an appropriate continuing professional development (CPD) programme. The programme is scheduled to run from November 2009 until September 2011 and will be made available, free of charge, to at least one teacher from every state-maintained secondary school in England.

From its inception, a very important consideration in the development of the HEDP was that its CPD programme should be built upon a rich and comprehensive research base. It had been identified as a key concern of The Pears Foundation and others working in this area that very little was known, or had been systematically recorded, at a national level about the extent and nature of teaching about the Holocaust in England or elsewhere within the UK. Therefore an early priority for the HEDP was to conduct a detailed and extensive investigation of teachers' practice and perspectives in this field. An online survey comprising 54 different questions was designed and advertised to secondary school teachers across England. The survey was accessible between November 2008 and February 2009 and received responses from 2,108 individuals. This was supplemented by in-depth, follow-up, small group interviews with 68 teachers visited at 24 different schools across the country.

This document reports on the key findings of this research.

---

[3] Within the UK, England, Scotland, Wales and Northern Ireland each have their own education departments whose organisation and funding is structured separately. The Holocaust Education Development Programme was mandated to focus its work on English secondary schools.

[4] Specifically, the Holocaust Education Development Programme (HEDP) is part of the Institute of Education (IOE), University of London and jointly funded by The Pears Foundation and the Department for Children, Schools and Families (DCSF) with support from the Holocaust Educational Trust (HET).

RESEARCH AIMS AND OBJECTIVES

The research was governed by four key aims:

1. To provide a more comprehensive empirical portrait of Holocaust education in English secondary schools than had previously existed.[5]

2. To investigate teachers' initial training and professional development in Holocaust education as well as their familiarity with and use of specialist organisations and/or resources in this field.

3. To examine individual teachers' personal and professional aims, approaches, understandings and knowledge base when teaching about the Holocaust.

4. To identify any particular challenges and/or opportunities encountered or perceived by teachers when teaching about the Holocaust.

The research was not established to identify or report on 'good practice' in schools, but rather to detail and describe the variety of approaches currently adopted and, where appropriate, to draw out some of the possible implications of these practices.

Because the Holocaust is currently a statutory component of the Key Stage 3 history curriculum, the HEDP's CPD programme was initially conceived to target secondary school history teachers. Although both the survey and follow-up interviews incorporated the viewpoints and experiences of teachers from other subject areas, this primary focus on history teaching impacted upon the design and analysis of the research and is reflected in its reporting here.

EXISTING RESEARCH ON TEACHING ABOUT THE HOLOCAUST IN ENGLISH SECONDARY SCHOOLS

In 2006, as a member country of the Task Force for International Cooperation on Holocaust Education, Remembrance and Research (ITF), the United Kingdom submitted a report on the provision of education about the Holocaust in British schools. At that time a number of the ITF's questions were considered 'impossible to answer' because there was insufficient research evidence from which to report (ITF 2006). The only existing national level survey of teachers' practice had been conducted prior to the introduction of the National Curriculum in 1987 (Fox 1989).

However, an important and growing body of research-informed literature in this area does exist. Indeed, a number of writers have conducted small-scale survey and/or interview based research, both with teachers (including, for example, Hector 2000; Russell 2006; Short & Reed 2004; Supple 1992) and with pupils (including, Maitles & Cowan 2007 and Short 2005). This

---

[5] Here the research was concerned to answer questions such as: Where in schools is the Holocaust being taught? By whom? Over how many hours? It was also concerned to explore the relationships between this empirical picture and the curricular and policy context in which teaching about the Holocaust is currently framed.

research has helped to identify a variety of salient issues and themes. For example, in their 1998 study, Brown and Davies reported an apparent confusion or lack of clarity among teachers over their aims when teaching about the Holocaust (see also Fox 1989). Russell (2006) built upon this observation suggesting that, within the group of history teachers that she interviewed, a tension or inconsistency often existed between the aims that were considered important or appropriate when teaching about the Holocaust and broader, disciplinary (here 'historical') aims. Clements (2006) also described uncertainty, doubt and confusion among both history and religious education teachers as to the 'practical outcomes' teachers wanted their students to achieve.

Research also has drawn attention to a number of recurring, potential challenges facing teachers in this area. Some of these appear as practical obstacles such as: insufficient curriculum time (Brown & Davies 1998; Hector 2000); limited opportunities for effective collaboration across departments (Brown & Davies 1998); and teachers who consider themselves 'under-informed' and/or 'under-resourced' (Supple 1992). Other researchers have described a variety of social, political and even philosophical concerns: How should teachers deal with students' prejudice, for example? What is an appropriate level of emotional engagement or objective neutrality? Is the Holocaust really ever possible to 'understand'? (Bauer, 2001; Burtonwood 2002; Carrington & Short 1997; Short 1994a).

While such prior research helped to frame and inform the design of both the HEDP survey and later interviews, many of the writers referenced above have themselves emphasised the small-scale and tentative nature of their work. The current report, therefore, represents an opportunity to examine these same issues and challenges in a manner unprecedented in either scope or scale, at least within the context of the UK. In 2008, the *Living History Forum* conducted a comparable, extensive national survey of teachers in Sweden, the first of its kind among the ITF's member nations (Lange 2008). Although there are significant differences between the Swedish and English contexts, the rationale and methodology of this Swedish survey has also informed the HEDP research.

WIDER CONTEXT OF THE RESEARCH

The Holocaust was first named as a topic for compulsory inclusion within secondary school history in England with the introduction of a statutory National Curriculum in 1991.[6] From the outset, this posed a daunting challenge to teachers due to the specific important, complex and sensitive concerns that the subject can raise; few teachers were operating with the advantage of professional training in this field and existing resources and support mechanisms were limited.

Since 1991, the Holocaust has 'featured with increasing prominence' (Russell 2006: 1) both within the school curriculum and within wider, popular consciousness, through the popularity of films like *Schindler's List* (originally released in 1993) and regular coverage in print and

---

[6] See Russell, 2006 for a detailed discussion of the background to the History Working Group's recommendation to the Secretary of State for Education that the Holocaust should be mandated in the history National Curriculum.

broadcast media (Russell *ibid*, Short & Reed, 2004).   The commitment and activity of organisations such as the British Friends of Yad Vashem, the Holocaust Educational Trust, the Anne Frank Trust, UK, The Holocaust Centre, the Imperial War Museum and the Jewish Museum London as well as individuals including Holocaust survivors and their families have also been significant in ensuring that the educational potential of studying the Holocaust is recognised.   Considerable funding has supported non-governmental organisations, museums and education centres in their work in this field. For example, the DCSF has funded the Holocaust Educational Trust's *Lessons From Auschwitz* project with £1.5 million a year since 2006 to enable two post-16 students from schools and sixth form colleges across England to take part in a programme of activities which include a one day visit to Auschwitz-Birkenau; permanent exhibitions are currently displayed at the Imperial War Museum, The Holocaust Centre in Laxton and the Jewish Museum, London; and, as of 2001, 27 January is now marked as an annual, national Holocaust Memorial Day.

The establishment of Holocaust Memorial Day also provides an important reminder that individual teachers' perspectives and practice when teaching about the Holocaust exist within a wider social, political and educational context.   Twenty-first century Britain comprises a rich and complex multicultural, social and political landscape.   Issues of 'social inclusion', 'community cohesion' and 'managing diversity' are high on the British Government's domestic agenda and in recent years this has significantly framed popular and political discussion of teaching about the Holocaust. This was highlighted by Burtonwood (2002: 71) when he noted that,

> In his Foreword to the [Holocaust Memorial] Consultation Day Paper, the Home Secretary placed the proposal for Holocaust remembrance within the context of a government vision of a multicultural society, within which individuals are encouraged to retain distinctive cultural identities while sharing a collective national identity.

It would not be appropriate or possible to capture the complexities inherent in encouraging 'collective national identity' within multicultural, multiethnic and multifaith-based societies in this report.   However, it is important to note that organisations such as the Community Security Trust, The All-Party Parliamentary Group against Antisemitism, UK Equalities and Human Rights Commission (previously the Commission for Racial Equality) and the Runnymede Trust continue to report examples of antisemitism, Islamophobia and other forms of racism and prejudice in British society and British schools (see, for example, CRE 2002; CST 2008, 2009; PCAA 2007, 2008).   Indeed, in July 2009, the Community Security Trust reported that they had recorded more antisemitic incidents across the UK in the first six months of 2009 than in any of the previous five full calendar years.   609 incidents had been recorded by the end of June 2009; the previous highest recorded annual figure was 598 incidents in 2006. Such incidents include 63 reports of damage and desecration of Jewish property, 391 categorised as abusive behaviour (for example, antisemitic graffiti on non-Jewish property, hate mail and verbal abuse) and 77 violent assaults.   48 incidents were directed at Jewish schoolchildren and/or Jewish schools (CST 2009).

Again, the complex nature and longevity of antisemitism – its persistence in various forms and expressions through 2,000 years of European history – is impossible to adequately outline here, but Foxman (2008), the Community Security Trust (*op cit.*) and others have noted that outbursts are especially likely to be elicited by periods of economic downturn and political unrest. Moreover, research by Short (1991; 1997) has suggested that antisemitism is not always adequately acknowledged or addressed within the antiracist frameworks commonly adopted by schools.

The research is also set within a context of current wider professional discourse about the teaching of history in schools. The National Curriculum for history has been revised three times since 1991. No single tradition or set of influences contributed to the original curriculum and as a consequence it has been very difficult to assert that there are a coherent set of aims and purposes for history education in England on which all can agree. At various times there have been both practical and conceptual priorities set for history education that range from inculcation into appropriate conceptual understandings to acquisition of the generic skill sets and competencies that some believe history education can provide. More recently there have been efforts to ally history with the relatively new curriculum addition of citizenship. This has been welcomed and resisted in equal measure. It is against this backdrop that individual teachers' understandings are formed and decisions for teaching practice are made (Crawford 1996; Dickinson 2000; Foster 1998; Haydn 2004; Howson 2009; Lee & Howson 2006; Phillips 1998; Shemilt 2009; Slater 1989; Sylvester 1994).

STRUCTURE OF THE REPORT

Following this introduction, Chapter 2 provides further detail of the methodology used within the online survey and follow-up interviews. It presents basic demographic information on the survey sample and the schools and teachers visited for interview and describes the statistical and interpretive analysis employed.

Chapter 3 draws primarily upon the survey data to offer an overview of national level trends in Holocaust education within English secondary schools. It reports on how many teachers in different subject areas appear to be teaching about the Holocaust, how many hours they are likely to spend with each year group, what professional development they have received, what topics they regularly include in their teaching, and what resources they most frequently report having used. The chapter also discusses existing statutory instruction for teaching about the Holocaust, and highlights the inclusion of the Holocaust within 2008-09 specifications for public GCSE and GCE (A Level) exams. As part of the HEDP research, it was considered important to cautiously examine teachers' subject knowledge in relation to the history of the Holocaust. However, accurately measuring and responsibly reporting 'knowledge levels' in *any* subject is an inherently complex and contentious task. For this reason, Chapter 3 closes with an expanded and in-depth commentary on the answers given by teachers to a series of knowledge-based questions included in the survey.

Chapter 4 moves from the macro level of national trends and statistics to explore the understandings, motivations and experiences of individual teachers in individual schools. Where Chapter 3 reports on *what* is going on in terms of teaching about the Holocaust, Chapter 4 attempts to examine *why* teachers do what they do. The chapter asks: Are teachers clear on the reasons why they teach about the Holocaust? Do they have specific teaching aims? And, do these aims vary depending upon the subject they teach? How do teachers understand or define the term 'the Holocaust? Is this something that teachers have had cause – or opportunity – to reflect upon? What are the relationships between teachers' aims, their definitions and their knowledge base?

Chapter 5 examines potential opportunities and challenges for teaching about the Holocaust, both for individual teachers and for the field of Holocaust education in general. Discussion here includes: time and other curriculum concerns, cross-curricular cooperation (or confusion), diversity within the classroom, pupil prejudice, relationships between staff and students, and access to specialist professional support.

The concluding chapter (Chapter 6) draws together the key findings of the HEDP's research, and considers their implication for supporting teachers through continuing professional development in this field.

Between November 2008 and February 2009, more than two thousand teachers in secondary schools across England responded to an online survey which invited them to share their experience and opinions on teaching about the Holocaust. 24 of these teachers, and an additional 44 of their colleagues, also participated in follow-up interviews.

CHAPTER 2: METHODOLOGY

INTRODUCTION

To meet the aims and objectives of this study, a mixed methodological approach was employed. As Figure 1 illustrates, the research was divided into two phases: phase 1 collected primarily quantitative data through a 54-question online survey accessed by 2,108 respondents; phase 2 comprised follow-up qualitative interviews with 68 teachers in 24 schools. An early research objective was to identify in exactly which subject areas the Holocaust was being taught. Although compulsory within Key Stage 3 history, existing small-scale research and the experience of Holocaust educators consulted in the first stages of the study had suggested that students may also encounter the Holocaust in other areas of the secondary school curriculum. For this reason, the research was designed in such a way that it was initially open to all secondary teachers, irrespective of their subject background. Furthermore, in order to engage with as wide an audience as possible – and as a guide to future lines of enquiry – teachers were invited to complete the survey whether or not they had any prior experience of teaching about the Holocaust. However, during phase 2 it was considered important to narrow the research focus to those with teaching experience in this area and in particular, to teachers of history. This chapter more fully outlines both phases of the research by explaining the target population, recruitment of participants, instrument design and methods of data analysis used.

All aspects of the research were conducted under the ethical guidelines of the British Educational Research Association (BERA 2004). Throughout the study, the confidentiality of respondents' views and personal details was protected and maintained. In the reporting that follows, the identity of all individuals and schools or colleges has been anonymised.

Research phase	Research method	Data collection period	Number of participants	Subject taught
Phase 1	Online survey	November 2008 - February 2009	2,108	Teachers from a wide range of subjects
Phase 2	Group interviews	March 2009 - April 2009	68 (from 24 schools)	54 history; 9 RE; 5 other

Figure 1: Overview of the research design

DEVELOPMENT OF THE RESEARCH

The research design and the data collection instruments – that is, the survey text and interview protocol – were informed by a meticulous six-month consultation, testing, and revision process. During this period a range of approaches were adopted and a number of individuals and organisations were consulted. In summary the process comprised:

- a systematic review of all existing research on Holocaust education

- ongoing consultation with professional educators, stakeholders and national and international experts in Holocaust education (see Appendix 2)

- consultation with Holocaust education agencies and related organisations (see Appendix 3)

- ongoing consultation with members of the HEDP Advisory Board (see Appendix 4)

- employing the quantitative and qualitative design expertise of senior researchers based at the Institute of Education

- a systematic and prolonged process of piloting with individual teachers and focus groups in July, September and October 2008 (survey instrument) and February 2009 (interview guide).

PHASE 1

Target population and recruitment of survey respondents

As indicated above, during the first phase of the research, a deliberate decision was taken to consider the perspectives and experiences of teachers from all curriculum areas in secondary schools across England, irrespective of whether or not they had taught about the Holocaust before. To this end it was considered that an open access online survey would be an effective research tool. A national, cross-subject publicity campaign was launched to raise teachers' awareness of the survey and to encourage them to take part. The campaign included:

- direct engagement with a broad range of subject associations, local authorities, and educational networks

- direct e-mail contact with all secondary schools in England through a purchased electronic database

- direct e-mail contact with head teachers through DCSF electronic newsletters

- utilisation of the comprehensive network of educators linked to the Institute of Education

- direct engagement with Holocaust organisations, museums, and agencies in the UK

- coverage in national newspapers (e.g., the *Guardian,* the *Telegraph,* the *Times Educational Supplement*)

- selective advertising in nationally circulated educational magazines and journals.

In addition, while it remained live and online, responses to the survey were systematically monitored and analysed. Secondary schools in local authorities that provided a low or zero response rate were directly contacted by telephone in an attempt to encourage greater completion.

The open invitation to all secondary school teachers was further supplemented by a more targeted approach. This focused on teachers in those subjects deemed most likely to include teaching about the Holocaust (on the basis or prior research and the experience of Holocaust education specialists consulted within the research). The targeted campaign included:

- direct e-mail contact with Heads of Humanities in secondary schools in England employing a targeted database

- advertising in professional magazines and journals (e.g., *Teaching History*)

- direct e-mail contact with 1500 named teachers listed as teaching citizenship, English, history, humanities, PSHE and RE

- direct engagement with relevant contacts and networks in targeted subject associations (e.g., citizenship, English, history, RE).

Survey instrument design and implementation

Following extensive piloting, the final version of the survey was hosted online as part of the HEDP website (http://www.hedp.org.uk). It remained live for a 13-week period from November 9, 2008 to February 10, 2009. The survey contained 54 separate questions to elicit a variety of factual and evaluative responses from teachers. For example, one question asked teachers to record how many hours they were likely to spend teaching about the Holocaust with individual year groups while another asked if there were any specific resources that they found particularly useful or effective when doing so. Most of the survey questions were closed questions in which teachers were asked to choose from a list of suggested responses or to indicate agreement/disagreement along a five-point Likert scale. A smaller number of open or free-text questions were also included for respondents to provide specific details or further commentary.

The structure of the survey took into account that not all respondents had prior experience of teaching about the Holocaust. Although designed to investigate the views, knowledge and understandings of *all* secondary school teachers, the survey did not require those teachers with no experience in this area to complete questions related to pedagogy, curriculum choices, training or knowledge of specialist organisations working in this field. These teachers were only directed to complete the first 35 and final five of the 54 questions included in the survey.

All teachers were asked about:

- their understandings of the Holocaust

- the aims they would prioritise if and when teaching about the Holocaust

- their perceived level of knowledge, preparedness and confidence in this area

- the extent to which their knowledge of the Holocaust was informed by books (other than textbooks), visits to memorial sites either in the UK or abroad and/or meetings with Holocaust survivors

- their actual historical knowledge of the Holocaust

- whether or not they had taught about the Holocaust before.

Where teachers *had* taught about the Holocaust, the survey then asked about:

- the subject(s) and year group(s) in which this teaching took place

- the amount of time allocated to the subject

- cooperation between different curriculum areas when teaching about the Holocaust

- teaching approaches and topic coverage

- any training they had received to help them teach about the Holocaust and their experience of and with specialist educational organisations in this field.

Where teachers had not taught about the Holocaust, they were asked to provide details of the reason(s) why.

All teachers were invited to provide any additional information or commentary about Holocaust education and asked if they would be interested in participating in further research.

Sample and representativeness

The 2,108 teachers who gave responses to the online survey represent an opportunity sample. As with any research derived from a *sample* of a target population, it would be inappropriate and irresponsible to claim to report here on the practice and perspectives of *all* teachers currently working in English secondary schools. However, the survey produced an extensive, rich and complex data set from which it is both possible and instructive to report apparent patterns in experience and potentially salient trends.

Furthermore, although the final achieved sample of an open survey of this nature can never be completely controlled, a number of measures were taken to encourage responses from an audience that reflected variation representative of the wider teaching population in geographic and demographic terms. Comparative analysis of the background information provided by the 2,108 respondents and national data held by the DCSF and General Teaching Council (GTC) suggests that the research was broadly successful in this respect as is documented below.

The majority of survey respondents were female (59%, n1,217) exactly mirroring the gender distribution of the wider secondary work force (Hansard 2009). A broad age range was represented – from 20 years of age to over 60 years of age – with the largest group concentrated between 26 and 30 years old (19%, n382). Figure 2 below illustrates the age range of respondents.

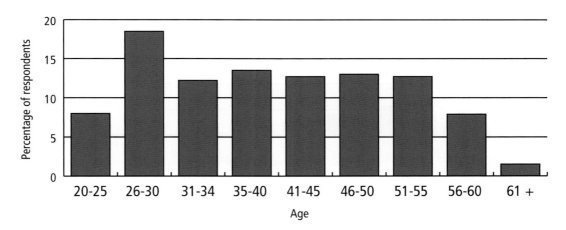

Figure 2: Age profile of survey respondents (n2,065)

The ethnicity of teachers was predominantly white (94%, n1,926) which is in line with DCSF school workforce data for January 2008.[7] Most respondents classified themselves as Christian (60%, n1,204) while 31% (n614) declared themselves adhering to no religion. A small number of respondents were Jewish (4%, n71), whereas even smaller numbers were Muslim (1%, n25), Hindu (0.3%, n6) and Buddhist (0.7%, n15).

Most respondents were in full-time employment (91%, n1,861), and the largest concentration of teachers who responded to the survey were those who began teaching between 2000 and 2007. The single largest group began teaching in 2004 (7%, n137). Responses were received from teachers who began their training as far back as 1962, with no contributions recorded for only three years (1963, 1964 and 1966).

The respondents were trained in a wide variety of subject areas. The most common subject of training was history (35%, n693), followed by religious education (18%, n353), English (9%, n182), and science (7%, n142). The majority of respondents described themselves as principally teachers of history (37%, n691), followed by religious education (19%, n360), and English (10%, n186), although, again, all subject areas were represented.

---

[7] DCSF, *School Workforce in England,* January 2008 (94% of all teachers employed in local authorities categorised themselves in terms of ethnicity as 'white').

Most respondents identified themselves as working in comprehensive schools (53%, n950), followed by community schools/colleges (14%, n251), or schools with a religious character (12%, n207). The type of school in which respondents taught is illustrated in Figure 3.

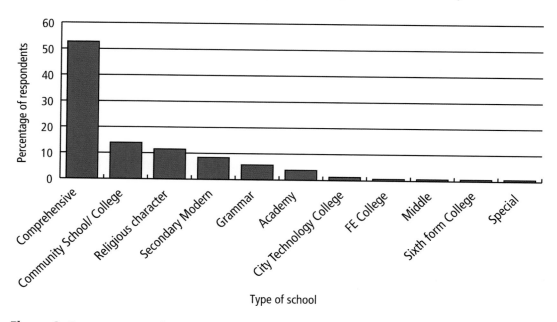

Figure 3: Survey respondents by school type (n1,803)

Teachers from most local authorities completed the survey with at least one return. The regions with the highest responses were the South East (19%, n364), London (19%, n361), and the South West (12%, n232).

Other regions with returns of 10% or below are included in Figure 4 which relates the approximate percentage of secondary teachers to each government office region and compares that to the regional concentration of responses to the survey.

Government Office Region	Number of secondary teachers[8]	Percentage of national total (England)	Number of survey respondents	Percentage of total survey respondents
North East	10.8	5.4	96	5
North West	28.4	14.3	180	9.3
Yorkshire and Humberside	20.5	10.3	148	7.6
East Midlands	17.6	8.8	125	6.4
West Midlands	22.6	11.4	180	9.3
East	22.6	11.4	195	10
London	26.5	13.3	361	18.6
South East	30.3	15.2	364	18.7
South West	19.6	9.9	232	11.9
Other[9]	-	-	61	3.1
Total	198.8	100	1,942	100

Figure 4: Representativeness of achieved survey sample by government office region (n1,942)

Figure 5 illustrates that the teachers who responded to the survey had a broad span of teaching experience ranging from newly qualified teachers (NQT) to one respondent with 54 years' experience. The largest single group of teachers who responded to the survey were those with four years of teaching experience (7%, n135). The group who provided the largest survey return included those teachers who had taught between one and five years (30%, n583).

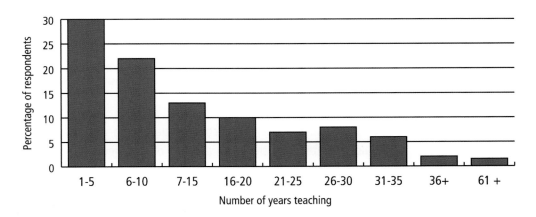

Figure 5: Survey respondents by duration of teaching experience (n1,941)

---

[8] These figures are for qualified teachers only and full-time equivalents in the state maintained sector in 2008.

[9] The survey asked teachers to identify in which local authority their school was situated. 61 teachers noted that they were either not in a recognized local authority or that it was not applicable (e.g. teachers who taught in academies).

Data analysis

Analysis of the online survey was undertaken using statistical software, notably SPSS Version 16. This facilitated data manipulation and also provided frequency reports, cross-tabulations and factor analyses. Analysis was also conducted on individual survey questions to assess the internal consistency of the data set as a further measure of reliability. In each case this resulted in a high or acceptable measure of internal consistency. Open text responses were also reviewed and, where appropriate, entered into NVIVO Version 8 for further coding and analysis.

Early comparative analysis was conducted on the basis of examining the survey data in two ways. The first approach was to examine all responses given by teachers who had taught about the Holocaust either during the last three years (58%, n1,038) or at some earlier point in their careers (9%, n155). The second way was to examine the responses given by those teachers who had never taught about the Holocaust (33%, n590). Figure 6 illustrates the responses of the 1,783 teachers who indicated whether they had taught about the Holocaust recently, previously or never before as the basis for classifying and investigating these two principal approaches.

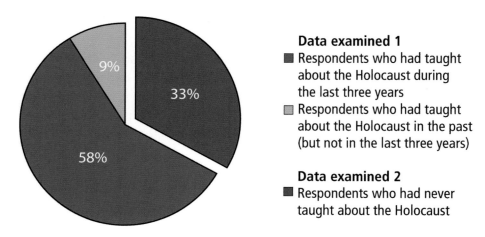

Data examined 1
■ Respondents who had taught about the Holocaust during the last three years
▦ Respondents who had taught about the Holocaust in the past (but not in the last three years)

Data examined 2
■ Respondents who had never taught about the Holocaust

Figure 6: Survey respondents prior experience in teaching about the Holocaust (n,1783)

Of course many other potential and instructive approaches to classifying and analysing the data exist. Moreover, it should be noted that the huge amount of data recorded and stored provides plentiful opportunities for ongoing research and evaluation in the future. To date, analysis has primarily focused on investigating those teachers who teach or have taught about the Holocaust. Of those with such experience, more than half stated that they taught about the Holocaust principally within history (55%, n591) and approximately one quarter did so principally within RE (25%, n269). Concentrations of teachers were also identified within English, citizenship and PSHE. These five subject areas are used as the basis of much of the comparative analysis reported here. However, it is important to note that while the survey has successfully captured large samples of teachers describing their practice within both history and RE, the numbers of respondents describing practice within English, citizenship and PSHE are considerably smaller and therefore claims to the representative nature of their responses are more tentative.

PHASE 2

Target population and recruitment of interviewees

While the online survey was an appropriate tool to capture a broad range of opinions and experience from a variety of different groups of teachers at a national level, it was also considered important to build upon this data by conducting follow-up interviews with teachers currently teaching about the Holocaust in English secondary schools. Given the initial remit of the research to award primary attention to the relevant compulsory component of the National Curriculum, history teachers were specifically targeted here.

A three-step process determined participants for the interviews. Firstly, the final question of the online survey asked teachers if they would be willing to be interviewed at a future date. 149 teachers positively responded to this request and a list was drawn up of volunteers who identified themselves as teachers of history. Second, a detailed analysis of the participants who had volunteered was undertaken. The objective of the analysis was to identify a cohort of interviewees broadly representative of the diverse range of schools and teachers in England (as is further detailed below). In order to ensure a geographic spread, teachers were selected from each of the nine government office regions (GORs) in a manner broadly related to the number of teachers in each region (see Figure 7).[10]

During the third step of the process, selected history teachers were contacted to arrange interviews at their respective schools. These teachers were also asked to arrange for two additional teachers to join the group interview. Teachers were requested to invite colleagues from within their history department with experience of teaching about the Holocaust. However, in schools where this proved difficult to organise, it was agreed that teachers who had taught about the Holocaust in other subject areas could participate. Of the 68 teachers who participated in the interviews 54 taught history, nine taught RE and five taught in other subject areas including citizenship, geography and combined humanities.

Interview design and implementation

Group interviews were conducted in 24 secondary schools across England during a period from March to April 2009. Lasting on average one hour, the interviews typically involved three teachers from each school. In total, 68 teachers participated in the interviews.

The interviews were intended to add depth and complexity to the survey data and to provide a greater opportunity for teachers to articulate their thoughts and experiences in their own words. A semi-structured interview guide was designed and developed on the basis of early analysis of the survey data to facilitate further exploration of apparent patterns and additional

---

[10] The nine Government Office Regions (GOR) are: North East, North West, Yorkshire and Humberside, East Midlands, West Midlands, East, London, South East, and South West.

questions that had begun to emerge. The interviews produced rich and detailed discussion around five key areas: teachers' definitions of the Holocaust; teaching aims; the practical 'nuts and bolts' of classroom activity; support from Holocaust education organisations; and challenges perceived or encountered in this area of work. Each interview was audio-recorded with the consent of all those teachers who took part.

Sample and representativeness

The 68 teachers who were interviewed constitute a purposive sample which grew from 24 individuals specifically targeted from among those who had volunteered to take part after completing the online survey. The subject background of these teachers has already been described. The balance between male and female teachers was almost equal (35 women and 33 men). A wide range of teaching experience was also reflected within the group: 11 interviewees were either in their NQT year or in their first years of teaching (i.e., between one and five years), whereas 16 interviewees indicated that they had been teaching for more than 20 years.

In selecting interviewees, considerable attention was given to ensure that teachers were included who taught in a broad range of schools. Accordingly, the schools that were visited for interview reflect appropriate variation in size, urban or rural location, the ethnic diversity of students and other socio-economic indicators such as the proportions of students who speak English as additional language and of those who receive free school meals. In addition, the sample was selected both to include single sex and co-educational schools as well as a variety of school types (e.g., comprehensive, secondary, grammar, academy, sixth form college).

As described previously and as depicted in Figure 7 below, the sample was also chosen to ensure a geographic spread of schools throughout the nine GORs: North East, North West, Yorkshire and Humberside, East Midlands, West Midlands, East, London, South East, and South West.

Region	Number of Schools
North East	2
North West	4
Yorkshire and Humberside	2
East Midlands	2
West Midlands	3
East	1
London	4
South East	3
South West	3

Figure 7: Regional distribution of 24 schools visited for interview

The 24 schools visited also reflect the broad range of academic achievement that exists across the country. While in two schools almost the entire school population achieved 5 GCSE grades of A to C or better in 2008, in five others, the same year's 'A to C' rate was below 40%.

Overall, therefore, although in this qualitative aspect of the study it would be inappropriate to claim that the sample was representative of all schools in England, it is reasonable to suggest that the sample population of interviewees and the schools in which they taught broadly reflects the diverse range of schools and school populations in existence across the country.

Data analysis

Initial analysis of the group interviews was informed by emergent findings derived from the online survey. Each one of the 24 interviews was fully transcribed and the interview content verified by the HEDP interviewer. Interviewer notes were also written up after interview and collated alongside any other pertinent information collected from the school (for example, details of lesson plans, schemes of work and/or specific exam board specifications). The full transcript of each interview was examined to identify key areas of consensus and contradiction and in order to capture the diversity of teachers' experiences and views. Text from each transcript was entered into NVIVO Version 8 for coding and further inductive analysis. Recurring themes, salient interpretations and potential tensions were highlighted and systematically compared and contrasted with the results of the online survey.

SUMMARY

In summary, the mixed methodological approach to the research provided a wealth of information in keeping with the specified aims and objectives of the investigation. The online sample of teachers and the in-depth interviews proved substantial in scope, scale and diversity. The online survey alone was based upon 2,108 teachers responding to 54 questions.[11] In addition, transcripts of the interviews for phase 2 resulted in more than 700 pages of text to be analysed. Furthermore, these group interviews added detail, complexity and richness to the emerging picture of how the Holocaust is taught in secondary schools in England. As a result of the selected methods and the data collection procedures employed, a systematic analysis and interpretation of a national data set of unprecedented proportions was made possible. The following chapters report extensively on the key findings which emerged from this substantial data set.

---

[11] It is also worth noting that the survey was closely monitored while it was live and there was no evidence of any malicious activity. Statistical checks and pattern analyses during and after the live phase were carried out and only 150 returns warranted investigation. These were subsequently found to be satisfactory although only partially completed.

Teachers teach about the Holocaust across all seven year groups of secondary education and in a wide variety of subject areas including history, religious education, English, citizenship and PSHE

The Holocaust is a compulsory part of the national curriculum within Key Stage 3 history. Students must be taught about:

> the changing nature of conflict and cooperation between countries and peoples and its lasting impact on national, ethnic, racial, cultural or religious issues, including the nature and impact of the two world wars and the Holocaust, and the role of European and international institutions in resolving conflicts.

(QCA 2007: 116)

CHAPTER 3: THE CURRENT LANDSCAPE OF HOLOCAUST EDUCATION IN ENGLISH SECONDARY SCHOOLS

INTRODUCTION

This chapter outlines the contours of the current landscape of Holocaust education in English secondary schools as suggested through analysis of the data captured by the online survey. It highlights the subject areas in which survey respondents most frequently reported teaching about the Holocaust and indicates the statutory and non-statutory guidelines which may frame these teachers' work. Five key subject areas – history, RE, English, citizenship and PSHE – are used as the basis for comparative analysis to reveal variation and/or convergence in the time spent, content included and pedagogical approach taken by teachers from different subject backgrounds. The responses given to a series of questions included in the survey to explore teachers' subject knowledge of the Holocaust are also discussed.

IN WHICH AREAS OF THE CURRICULUM DOES TEACHING ABOUT THE HOLOCAUST TAKE PLACE?

As has already been described in Chapter 2, 1,193 of the 2,108 teachers who completed the online survey reported that they were teaching or had taught about the Holocaust now or at some point in their careers (of these, 1,038 said they had done so within the past three years). This group was then asked within which subject this teaching principally took place. 1,084 chose to answer and their responses are shown in Figure 8.

55% (n591) of these teachers said that they principally taught about the Holocaust within history classes, 25% (n269) said they taught about the Holocaust principally in religious education, 7% (n72) within English and 3% (n34 and n33) in each of citizenship and PSHE. The only two other subjects named by more than 10 respondents were modern foreign languages and drama with 16 and 12 individual responses (each constituting approximately 1%) respectively.

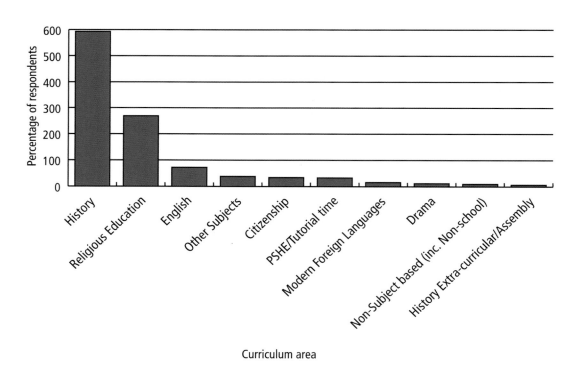

Figure 8: Curriculum areas in which survey respondents principally taught about the Holocaust (n1,084)

Teachers were also asked to indicate any additional subjects in which they taught about the Holocaust. Here, 485 teachers reported that they taught about the Holocaust in at least one other subject area. The responses given to both questions can be combined to reflect the total number of times each subject was indicated as an area in which the Holocaust was being taught about in schools (see Figure 9). This is instructive because it reveals that, in aggregate, a total of 176 teachers reported teaching about the Holocaust within citizenship and 167 within PSHE.[12]

---

[12]   Given the already extensive scope of the survey instrument, it was not practical to collect detailed information on teachers' practice outside of the principal subject that each individual identified. Supplementary research could instructively be conducted to enable a more detailed examination of teachers' practice within citizenship and PSHE classrooms than has been possible here.

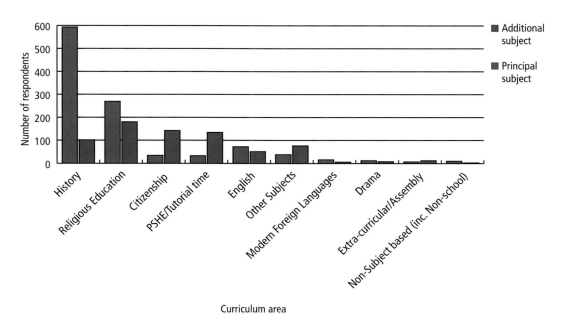

Curriculum area

Figure 9: All curriculum areas in which survey respondents taught about the Holocaust (n1,084)

Of note, by aggregating these figures, citizenship and PSHE appear as the third and fourth subjects in which the Holocaust is most likely to be taught, while English stands fifth. Among the 'other subjects' recorded here, small numbers of teachers reported that they taught about the Holocaust within a variety of different and perhaps unexpected subject areas including philosophy, psychology, science, maths, ICT and business studies as well as general studies and combined humanities. The survey also received responses from a small number of individuals whose teaching about the Holocaust was not subject-based - such as special educational needs co-ordinators – or was concentrated in extra-curricular activities, including school assemblies.

In addition, 590 teachers completed the survey who had *never* previously taught about the Holocaust. Of these, most explained that it was not an expected topic for inclusion within their specific subject(s). However, some made the point that outside of their planned schemes of work or programmes of study, unanticipated topics for discussion among students could emerge. As one mathematics teacher explained:

> Whilst not actually teaching about the Holocaust I will discuss it with students if they should bring the subject up - particularly as I have a Jewish surname. I have enough common sense and background knowledge to be able to allow discussion and challenge 'wrong' ideas in a sensitive manner.

> Extract from survey response

Other teachers suggested that they were not comfortable venturing into discussion of a topic that they considered would be best handled by 'subject specialists'. Some teachers also made a distinction between 'referring to' the subject as distinct from actually '*teaching* about it'.

STATUTORY REQUIREMENTS AND EXAM SPECIFICATIONS

Key Stage 3

History is currently the only subject within which the Holocaust is a compulsory part of the National Curriculum in English secondary schools. History teachers are directed to teach about the Holocaust during Key Stage 3, within the first three years of students' secondary education (Years 7, 8 and 9) between the ages of 11 and 14. Specifically, the 2007 curriculum highlights five aspects of British history and two of European and world history which comprise the 'Range and Content' which must be covered by all students in Key Stage 3. In the context of European and world history, the history National Curriculum mandates that students should be taught about,

> the impact of significant political, social, cultural, religious, technological and/or economic developments and events on past European and world societies,

and,

> the changing nature of conflict and cooperation between countries and peoples and its lasting impact on national, ethnic, racial, cultural or religious issues, including the nature and impact of the two world wars and the Holocaust, and the role of European and international institutions in resolving conflicts.

QCA 2007: 116, emphasis added

At present no comparable compulsory National Curriculum for religious education exists. Instead, the content for study at Years 7, 8 and 9 are suggested within a framework of locally agreed syllabi, responsibility for which lies within individual local authorities. Nevertheless, the Qualifications and Curriculum Authority has produced an exemplar Key Stage 3 programme of study. This references the Holocaust as an example of a topic that could be used to 'explor[e] human experiences such as suffering' and 'raise questions about people's abiding sense of meaning in the face of pain and fear' (QCA 2007: 269).

Citizenship is also a compulsory area of the curriculum at both Key Stages 3 and 4. While the National Curriculum guidelines for citizenship do not make direct reference to the Holocaust, the key concepts listed for the subject are, 'Democracy and Justice', 'Rights and Responsibilities' and 'Identity and Diversity'. A study of the Holocaust could clearly be considered relevant in the case of each of these.

Key Stage 4 and 5

In Years 10 and 11, students are able to choose between different General Certificate of Secondary Education (or GCSE) courses. In England in 2008, approximately 636,700 school students attempted at least one GCSE examination. Of these, approximately 204,000 attempted GCSE history (DCSF 2008b).

In England, three examination boards produce specifications for each GCSE. In the case of history, each exam board then offers a choice of at least three different specifications which schools could pursue. And so, during the academic year 2008/2009, 10 different specifications for GCSE history were available to students in English secondary schools. 'The Holocaust', or 'the Final Solution' was directly referred to within options for study in five of these. Figure 10 details the number of students entered for each specification in June 2008 and highlights if and where a reference to the Holocaust or 'the Final Solution' was made.

Specification	No. of entries	Details
A (3041) Schools' History Project	18,434	'The persecution of the Jews' and 'The Final Solution' are both listed as content for inclusion within the 'Enquiry in Depth' option 'Germany 1919-1945' (one of four options, one must be chosen).
B (3042) Modern World	45,355	There is no mention of 'The Final Solution' but 'The Holocaust, 1939-1945' is listed within the content focus of a unit on The Arab Israeli Conflict, one of three units that can be studied and examined in place of assessed coursework. The Arab Israeli Conflict is also listed alongside 'Anti-Semitism in The Twentieth Century', 'Germany' and 'The Second World War' among 14 suggestions for the focus of World History coursework. 'Germany 1918-1939' is included as one of four possible depth studies (two of four must be chosen).
C (3043) British Social & Economic History	766	No reference
A (1334) Modern European & World History	25,824*	The depth study, 'Nazi Germany, 1930-39' includes reference to 'persecution of the Jews'. (2 depth studies must be chosen from an available seven).
B (1335) Aspects of Modern Social, Economic & Political History	3,451*	Students must submit coursework on EITHER a study of British History OR a study of European or World History, and 'Weimar and Nazi Germany, c1919-1945' is one of seven possible choices within European or World History. The specification does not make direct reference to the Holocaust nor 'The Final Solution' but does include 'The persecution of Jews and other minorities' within Nazi Germany, 1933-1945.
C (1336) Schools' History Project	26,838*	'Germany c1919 – c1945' is one of three available in-depth enquiries (one must be chosen) although the Holocaust, 'Final Solution', and/or persecution of the Jews is not mentioned directly here. 'The "Final Solution" and its implementation across Europe' is listed as content within the coursework option, 'The economic and social impact of Nazi government' (one of nine that schools may choose) – however alternative coursework routes are also available.
A (1935) Schools' History Project	31,477	'The Final Solution' is included within the depth study, 'Germany c1919-45'. (one depth study must be chosen from five).
B (1937) Modern World	50,473	'The Final Solution' is included within the depth study, 'Germany c1919-45'. (one depth study must be chosen from four).
C (1936) British Social and Economic	1,957	No reference
Pilot	1,923	No reference

Figure 10: Figure 10: GCSE history entries, June 2008

* provisional figures only as of September 2008 (These figures have been compiled from statistical sources available on the AQA, Edexcel and OCR websites).

To add to the complexity of exam choices, secondary schools in England can alternatively choose to enter their students for examinations set by the WJEC (Welsh Joint Education Committee). The WJEC offers two GCSE history specifications. 'The Final Solution' is included within options for study in both of these. However, as it was not possible to collate reliable statistics for the number of entrants from English secondary schools for these specifications, they have not been included here.

It is also important to note that, even where neither the Holocaust nor 'the Final Solution' was explicitly referenced within a specification, teachers in some of the schools visited for interview often explained that they regularly made a personal decision to include it within their GCSE teaching anyway:

> For the GCSE, I don't actually have to teach up to the Holocaust. Don't have to do that but I do, because I just don't feel like I can leave it out. So we look at, domestically at Germany and at the Nazi racial policy but we actually only go to the outbreak of the Second World War. So, the actual full scale slaughter of Jews didn't take place until the invasion of the Soviet Union. So, I go on and I spend a lesson, where I talk about how that went on and the resources we've got are just excellent, so I can use those resources to do that. I sometimes spend two lessons doing that, because it's that much, but I really shouldn't be doing it, because... I'm taking away from the syllabus so it's not going to [count towards their exams].
>
> History and RE teacher, North West

A smaller number of students study for GCE Advanced, or A level, examinations in their final, post-compulsory years of college or school. In 2008 in England, approximately 42,110 16-18 year old students sat A level history (as a point of comparison, 80,860 and 57,620 students sat English and mathematics respectively (DCSF 2008c)). The Holocaust was included for possible study in all four A level history specifications offered by English examination boards in 2008/09. Although neither the Holocaust nor 'the Final Solution' are referred to within the WJEC A level syllabus, the specification offers a number of opportunities for students to explore the persecution of the Jews in Nazi Germany during 1933-45.

Within religious education, the Holocaust is included in the specifications of five of eight current GCSE courses and all three for A level exams. In English schools and colleges in 2008, there were approximately 16,850 entrants for A level religious education and 164,000 for GCSE (DCSF 2008b; DCSF 2008c).

AT WHAT AGES ARE STUDENTS TAUGHT ABOUT THE HOLOCAUST?

The online survey asked teachers *when* they taught about the Holocaust in terms of individual academic years. 992 of the 1,193 teachers who said they had experience in this area provided information. Figure 11 illustrates that teaching about the Holocaust takes place throughout secondary schooling with a clear concentration in Year 9, the final year of Key Stage 3. 76% of the 992 respondents reported that they taught about the Holocaust during this academic year.

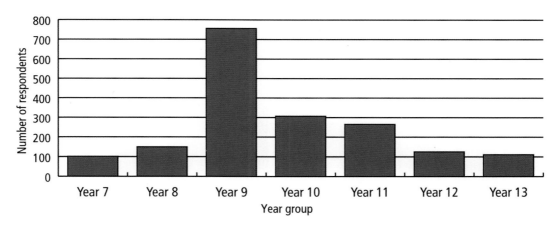

Figure 11: Year groups in which survey respondents principally teach about the Holocaust (n992)

As Figure 12 illustrates, the survey also suggests that relatively few teachers teach about the Holocaust to more than two different year groups within an academic year. Only 16 teachers reported teaching about the Holocaust to six different year groups or more and the highest proportion of teachers taught about it to only one year group.

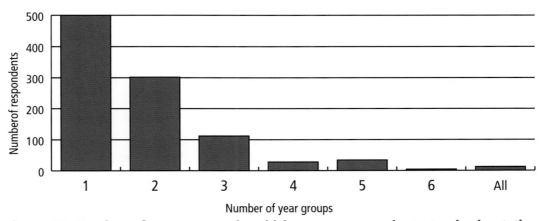

Figure 12: Number of year groups in which survey respondents teach about the Holocaust (n992)

It is also possible to examine variation in the year group structures of the different subjects within which teaching about the Holocaust takes place. Figure 13 illustrates the total number of teachers who report teaching about the Holocaust within each year group, split by the principal subject in which this teaching takes place. This figure suggests that it is only in Year 9 that history becomes the dominant subject for teaching about the Holocaust. Before Year 9, if a student has been introduced to the Holocaust during their school career, it is likely to have taken place in a subject other than history.

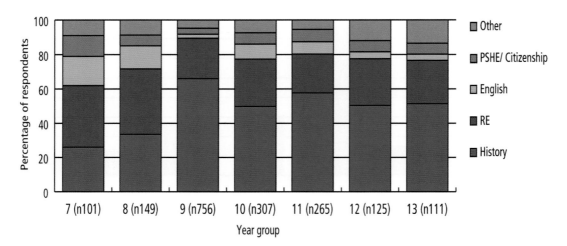

Figure 13: Teaching about the Holocaust by principal subject and year group.[13]

The concentration of teaching about the Holocaust within history and in Year 9 offers encouragement that, in the broadest terms at least, statutory curriculum requirements are being met. Only a very small number of history teachers reported that they had never taught about the Holocaust. Of these, most were newly qualified and in their first year of teaching and typically explained that they would be teaching about the Holocaust at a later stage of the academic year.

Widespread agreement existed among the history teachers interviewed that Year 9 was the most appropriate point to teach about the Holocaust within Key Stage 3. Many argued that it was 'a topic that demands maturity' or suggested that they needed time to develop trusting relationships with their students. Others explained that, in their schools, the content of Key Stage 3 history was taught 'chronologically' and as a consequence, the Holocaust was most likely to be encountered in students' final compulsory term. Yet the survey revealed a small group of 24 history teachers who reported that they *only* taught the Holocaust within Key Stage 3 history during Years 7 and/or 8. As one Head of History explained during interview, it is possible that in these schools, history was being 'cut back on' in terms of curriculum time and was not being taught in Year 9 at all. This was currently true in at least one of the schools visited for interview while in another no history was taught to students in Year 7. In a third school teachers described how they had created a Year 9 'taster' course for GCSE history, entitled *From Prejudice to Genocide*, in response to similar pressures on their curriculum time:

> **Teacher A**: [The taster course] is for GCSE, that's the idea, but the reality is, if we're honest, it's because we were suddenly expected to teach the whole of Key Stage 3 in two years and we were finding we just couldn't cram it into two years. So we decided, well, what topics are really powerful and very important and we'll move two of them into the Year 9 taster course.
>
> **Teacher B**: And also, it's because of the age as well. We were very reluctant to try and teach [the Holocaust] to the Year 8s.
>
> **Teacher A**: Yes. Yes. Because we used to teach both [slavery and the Holocaust] in Year 9.

---

[13] Due to the small number of teachers who reported that their teaching about the Holocaust took place principally within citizenship or PSHE, the figures have been aggregated here.

Teacher B: Yeah, we felt that Year 9 was the best place for it. So it would have to become part of our taster course.

History teachers, North West

Recent research reported by Wilson (2009) suggests that across England, more and more schools appear to be reducing the total time allocated for students to spend on history at Key Stage 3.

HOW MANY HOURS ARE SPENT TEACHING ABOUT THE HOLOCAUST?

Teachers who currently (or had previously) taught about the Holocaust were asked to indicate the number of hours they were likely to spend on the subject with each year group during a single academic year. The National Curriculum statutory guidelines do not stipulate how many hours should be spent teaching about the Holocaust. The survey reports considerable variation within each subject, year group and Key Stage. For example, among the 497 survey respondents who teach about the Holocaust within Year 9 history, 13 reported spending one hour each year doing so, while 16 reported spending 20 hours or more. Of these 497 responses, teachers most commonly reported spending six hours (75 respondents), four hours (71 respondents), five hours (54 respondents) or 10 hours (52 respondents) when teaching about the Holocaust during Year 9.

A more detailed description of the distribution of hours across year groups within specific subjects is provided in Figure 14. Some points of clarification are perhaps instructive here. The table records the total average, or 'mean' number of hours reported within each year group as well as the middle value, or 'median'. The table also indicates the range of hours spent on teaching about the Holocaust in any given year group. It reveals, for example, that whereas some teachers appear to spend one hour teaching about the Holocaust, some teachers devote 80 curriculum hours to the subject.

The survey data suggests that, when calculated across all year groups, more hours are spent teaching about the Holocaust by individual history teachers than by teachers from any other subject group. This remains consistent within individual year groups with the exceptions of Years 7 and 8. English teachers spend on average more hours than history teachers with both year groups as do citizenship teachers in Year 7. There is also greatest variation between the hours spent with different year groups among teachers of history.

	Across all years	Year 7	Year 8	Year 9	Year 10	Year 11	Year 12	Year 13
Citizenship								
No. of responses	60	7	7	14	13	14	3	2
Mean	5.3	3	3.6	5	5.3	5.2	10.3	15
Median	3	1	2	3	3	4	5	15
Range	1-25	1-10	1-10	1-20	1-25	1-25	1-25	5-25
English								
No. of responses	110	17	20	18	27	19	5	4
Mean	4.4	6	6.3	5.2	3.2	2.2	3.6	3
Median	3	4	3.5	2.5	2	2	4	2.5
Range	1-30	1-20	1-30	1-16	1-14	1-5	1-6	1-6
History								
No. of responses	999	26	50	497	153	153	63	57
Mean	7.8	2.9	5.5	7.2	7.6	6.4	10.8	17.6
Median	5	2	4	6	4	4	5	9
Range	1-80	1-12	1-20	1-40	1-76	1-76	1-70	1-80
Religious studies								
No. of responses	478	36	57	178	85	60	34	28
Mean	5.2	1.8	4.9	6.8	4.2	3.9	3.8	7.3
Median	4	2	4	6	3	3	3	4.5
Range	1-40	1-5	1-15	1-40	1-25	1-25	1-15	1-28
PSHE								
No. of responses	40	4	2	12	6	5	5	5
Mean	3.1	1.4	1.5	3.8	3.3	4	3	2.4
Median	2	1	1.5	3.5	2.5	1	3	2
Range	1-15	1-2	1-2	1-7	1-10	1-15	1-5	1-5

Figure 14: Amount of hours spent teaching about the Holocaust by subject area and year group (n992)

In the schools visited for interview, all history teachers reported spending a minimum of 'two or three' lessons (on average approximately an hour long) specifically on the Holocaust in Key Stage 3. Again, most reported spending at least five or six lessons and many spent eight or more. In one school, more than half of the 20 hour-long lessons devoted to history in Year 9 were spent on teaching about the Holocaust.

The interviews also revealed considerable variation in the number of hours spent teaching about the Holocaust with year groups 11 and 12 for GCSE. Teachers explained that this was largely a function of the exam specifications and coursework options chosen by the school. For example, teachers at one school calculated that, in total, they taught about the Holocaust within 20 GCSE history lessons.[14] For the majority of teachers interviewed, however, GCSE history offered less curriculum time and space for teaching about the Holocaust than Key Stage 3.

---

[14] Teachers in this school indicated they were able to do this by choosing to study the status and position of Jews in Europe between 1870 and 1917 and then again between 1933 and 1945 for their students' coursework options alongside a depth study on Germany 1918-1939 from the AQA Modern World Syllabus (B).

A smaller number of the schools visited for interviews offered a GCE A level history programme which included teaching about the Holocaust. In one school where this was the case, almost the entire academic year in Year 12 was spent delivering an AQA unit of work entitled, 'Anti-Semitism, Hitler and the German People, 1919-1942'.

In addition to the hours they spent teaching about the Holocaust within timetabled lessons, many of the teachers interviewed described additional Holocaust related activity that they were involved in or that happened within their school. Many reported that Holocaust Memorial Day was often marked by Holocaust related assemblies and associated whole school activities. Some schools appeared to be very involved in commemorating the Holocaust within their extended communities or at the level of local authorities. A number of teachers also described school visits organised to take students to museums and/or Holocaust memorial sites. In one school, teachers emphasised that a considerable amount of time was spent 'out of class time' preparing students for such visits.

WHAT CONTENT IS INCLUDED IN TEACHING ABOUT THE HOLOCAUST AND WHAT PEDAGOGICAL APPROACHES DO TEACHERS TAKE?

As part of the online survey, those teachers who had already reported that they had experience in this area were presented with a list of 35 possible topics that could be incorporated into a study of the Holocaust. This full list of topics is provided in Appendix 5. Teachers were asked to indicate which topics *they* included in their teaching, marking each along a five-point scale from those they 'never' included to those they would 'always' include. Appendix 5 ranks all 35 topics on the basis of how frequently each was reportedly taught.

Irrespective of teachers' subject background, the five topics that teachers were most likely to include were:

- the experiences of individual men, women and children who were persecuted by the Nazis, 88% (n900)

- Auschwitz-Birkenau, 87% (n875)

- propaganda and stereotyping, 78% (n801)

- *Kristallnacht*, 70% (n701)

- the choices and actions of bystanders, 66% (n671).

Approximately 60% of all respondents were more likely than not to teach about:

- the Nuremberg Laws (n606)

- the choices and actions of rescuers (n604)

- the study of Hitler's rise to power and the Nazi State (n600)

- combating current racist ideology (n595).

At the other end of the scale, irrespective of their subject background, considerably fewer teachers included the following topics in their teaching:

- the impact of the Holocaust on *The Declaration of Human Rights* (27%, n262)

- Jewish social and cultural life before 1933 (26%, n 260)

- the contribution of the Jews to European social and cultural life before 1933 (25%, n256)

- Operation Reinhard (12%, n119).

Analysis of this list and closer examination of teachers' topic choices offers a number of insights into pedagogical practice. It also points to some possible areas of concern. For example, many Holocaust educators would be troubled by the apparent lack of emphasis on Jewish life and culture before the war. Most experts in the field argue with conviction that it is impossible for students to understand the devastating impact of the Holocaust unless they have an awareness of what was lost and destroyed, and that any understanding of the significance of the Holocaust must include an appreciation of how Europe was transformed by the destruction of centuries-old Jewish communities throughout the continent (for a fuller discussion, see the ITF Education Working Group's *Guidelines for Teaching*, 2004).

Another concern is that the choice of topics might indicate a tendency to regard the victims of the Holocaust more as objects rather than as subjects of study – a passive mass of people to whom things were done, rather than individuals actively responding to the unfolding genocide. This is a tentative conclusion and requires further research: much depends on what teachers mean when they state that they include 'the experiences of individual men, women and children who were persecuted by the Nazis'. But given the high ranking of topics such as Auschwitz-Birkenau, propaganda and stereotyping, *Kristallnacht*, the Nuremberg Laws, Hitler's rise to power and the Nazi state, and the relatively low rankings of life in the ghettos, the Warsaw ghetto uprising, Jewish resistance in the camps and the actions of Jewish partisans, it appears that a perpetrator narrative predominates. It may be that the 'experiences of individual men, women and children' referred to primarily take the form of descriptions of what was done *to* Jewish people rather than how they responded. Moreover, the relatively high rankings of the choices of bystanders and of rescuers compared to topics that focus on the choices and actions of the victims may indicate greater attention to non-Jewish actors.

Furthermore, the high ranking of topics that relate to the events of the 1930s (Hitler's rise to power and the Nazi state; propaganda and stereotyping; *Kristallnacht*, the Nuremberg Laws) perhaps reflects a longstanding tendency in schools to focus on the Nazi period up to the outbreak of the Second World War. While the perpetrator narrative then appears to predominate, actual topics seem to centre largely on the period of persecution during the 1930s (and Auschwitz-Birkenau) rather than on key aspects in the development of the Holocaust during the war years. The Wannsee Conference and the mass murders by the *Einsatzgruppen* are only the 21st and 22nd most likely topics to be taught; Operation Reinhard - the programme to murder some two million Jews in the German-occupied part of Poland known as the General Government, which resulted in the gassing of some 1.7 million Jewish people in the death camps of Belzec, Sobibor and Treblinka II - is, bar one, the least likely topic to be taught in English schools.

Some topics revealed particularly pronounced variation between respondents depending on the subject in which their principal teaching about the Holocaust took place. For example, as Figure 15 illustrates, whereas large numbers of history teachers were likely to include topics such as National Socialist ideology, the Nuremberg Laws and *Kristallnacht*, these topics were less likely to be chosen by teachers of English and RE. Similarly, although the concept of suffering was selected by large numbers of RE teachers and some English teachers, it was not likely to be included by those who taught about the Holocaust within history.

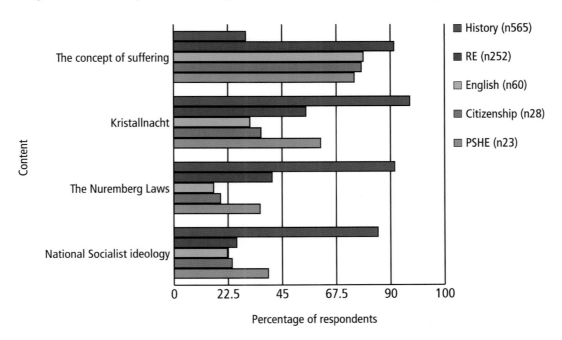

Figure 15: Subject based variation in content likely to be included in teaching about the Holocaust

The school-based interviews also provided an important opportunity to explore the reasons why individual teachers selected certain topics and these will be examined in further detail in Chapter 4. It is worth noting, however, that while GCSE and GCE A level exam specifications may provide a clear framework for content to be covered, within history at Key Stage 3, these decisions are not always easily made. As one London-based history teacher remarked, 'it is particularly difficult for Year 9 to know what to include and what to leave out'.

Within the survey data, there does not appear to be a particularly pronounced relationship between whether or not a topic is likely to be included and the total number of hours an individual teacher is able to spend teaching about the Holocaust; nor the year group and/or key stage in which their teaching takes place. The choices that teachers make here do not appear to be very clearly correlated to the time at their disposal, nor the age and/or prior familiarity with the Holocaust of the students that they teach.

Another survey question presented respondents with 26 statements about possible pedagogical practice when teaching about the Holocaust and asked them to indicate to what extent they agreed or disagreed with each. The full list of statements is reproduced in Appendix 1 (see question 41). Of the 1,053 teachers who responded to the statement 'I try to give students key facts and information about the Holocaust, providing them with a clear narrative outline' 87% (n917) said they agreed or strongly agreed. This was particularly pronounced among history teachers of whom 93% (n542) agreed[15] compared with 75% (n47) of English teachers and 74% (n23) of citizenship teachers. In fact, 13% (n4) of citizenship teachers said they actively disagreed.

Regardless of their subject background, a clear majority of all teachers agreed or strongly agreed that, 'when teaching about the Holocaust I allow time for debate and discussion' (92%, n974); 92% (n530) of history teachers; 95% (n249) of RE teachers; 92% (n61) of English teachers; and 87% (n26) of teachers of citizenship. Many teachers also agreed that they 'use testimony and individual stories to encourage students to engage with this subject on an empathetic level'[16] (91%, n955). However, there was slightly more variation between subjects here: while 93% (n537) and 93% (n242) of history and RE teachers agreed, only 74% (n49) of English teachers did. 88% (n925) of all teachers agreed that, 'when teaching about the Holocaust I ask students to consider moral and/or ethical questions'. This was also true of 83% (n481) of history teachers and 97% (n254) of RE teachers.

72% (n754) of all teachers agreed that, 'when teaching about the Holocaust I emphasise the horror of these events and the human suffering – I want students to have a deep emotional response to this topic'. This appeared to be particularly important for English teachers among whom 84% (n56) agreed, compared with 70% (n404) of history teachers and 61% (n19) of citizenship teachers.

Subject-specific variation also existed among those teachers who agreed that:

- 'when teaching about the Holocaust I engage students in political questions about power and/or the abuse of power' - 67% (n703) of all teachers, 73% (n420) of history teachers, 64% (n40) of English teachers, 55% (n141) of RE teachers and 50% (n15) of those who teach about the Holocaust within citizenship

- 'when teaching about the Holocaust I take an enquiry-based approach and work to address big questions' - 61% (n631) of all teachers, 66% (n378) of history teachers, 65% (n166) of RE teachers, 45% (n14) of citizenship teachers and 39% (n24) of English teachers

- 'when teaching about the Holocaust I adopt a source-based "skills" approach' - 41% (n419) of all teachers, 48% (n274) of history teachers and 58% (n18) of citizenship teachers compared with 34% (n84) of RE teachers and 15% (n19) of English teachers

---

[15] For the purposes of reporting here 'agreed' or 'disagreed' refers to the combined number of respondents who either agree/strongly agree or disagree/strongly disagree respectively unless otherwise specified.

[16] In fact the notion of 'historical empathy' has been the subject of much academic and practitioner debate (see, for example, Davis, Yeager, and Foster (eds). 2001; Harris and Foreman-Peck 2004).

- 'when teaching about the Holocaust I ask students to consider theological questions' - 35% (n355) of all teachers, 78% (n201) of RE teachers compared with 19% (n106) of history teachers.

The majority of all teachers were more likely to disagree than agree with the statement, 'when teaching about the Holocaust I start with students' perceptions and understandings of the Jewish community today' - 29% (n297) agreed while 44% (n449) disagreed. A similar balance of opinion was reported across all subjects with the exception of RE teachers among whom 40% (n102) agreed, while 27% (n76) disagreed.

Even fewer teachers agreed that 'when teaching about the Holocaust I take a disciplinary approach and focus on historical teaching' - 22% (n222) of all teachers, 31% (n172) of history teachers, 19% (n6) of citizenship teachers, 10% (n25) and 5% (n3) of RE and English teachers respectively.

WHAT RESOURCES DO TEACHERS USE?

Teachers taking part in the survey were invited to provide details of up to three resources that they found particularly useful or effective in their teaching about the Holocaust. Where more than one resource was listed teachers were asked to prioritise these in order of their value and effectiveness. 527 chose to list at least one resource and in total, 1,187[17] contributions were made. However, rather than provide details of an individual named resource, many respondents offered a contribution which described a particular type of resource, for example 'fiction or autobiographical works', 'documentary DVDs' or 'personal testimonies'.

In terms of individually named resources, the film *Schindler's List* was the most frequently cited, both among the most highly prioritised resources and in aggregate terms: 127 teachers named *Schindler's List* and among these 51 chose it as their first (most useful) resource. Specific teaching materials produced by the Imperial War Museum and Holocaust Educational Trust, and in particular the IWM's *Reflections* and HET's *Recollections* packs, were among the next most commonly named resources: *Reflections* was identified or described by 67 teachers and materials produced by HET by 45. The Diary of Anne Frank (in both book and film format) was named by 54 teachers within the survey.

Teachers were also asked to respond to a list of statements about the different sorts of resources used in their classroom, as illustrated in Figure 16. While 76% (n765) of all teachers said they were likely to use feature films about the Holocaust, 81%, (n814) reported that they were likely to use documentaries. Within interview, *Schindler's List* and more recent films such as *The Pianist* and *The Boy in the Striped Pyjamas* were regularly mentioned by teachers but so too were documentaries such as *Genocide,* an episode from the 1973 *World at War* Thames Television series, and, in 1997, *The Nazis – A Warning from History: The Road to Treblinka*

---

[17] On several occasions survey respondents named more than one resource or type of resource within a single contribution or provided an entry which could have been classified in various different ways.

(BBC). These documentaries were named by 31 and 18 teachers who took part in the survey respectively.

Although some of the teachers who were interviewed made occasional reference to textbooks, most suggested that they found audiovisual materials including photographs and archival footage particularly effective and/or popular with students. Where teachers did talk about the value of written texts, this tended to be the use of first person testimony, personal stories and/or eye-witness accounts. These same sorts of resources were also frequently prioritised within the survey. 115 respondents made a generalised reference to 'personal accounts' or 'eye witness testimony' and, in particular, '*survivors*' stories'. For 78 teachers these were listed as their first most useful and/or effective resource.

As Figure 16 also shows, 73% (n704) of survey respondents who provided detail here also described using resources they had developed themselves. The survey data suggests that fewer than one in five teachers were likely to use the Qualifications and Curriculum Authority's suggested schemes of work (18%, n172). Furthermore, relatively few teachers were likely to incorporate visits to a memorial site, research centre or museum outside of the UK (20%, n188) or invite experts and/or guest speakers to talk about the Holocaust (16%, n150). Less than a third of all respondents said they were likely to incorporate visits to a memorial site, research centre or museum within the UK (28%, n274). Approximately one quarter said they were likely to invite a Holocaust survivor to talk to students (25%, n248) in their schools. Of course, this does not mean that teachers do not value the work of these individuals or organisations. On the contrary, the value of hearing survivor stories in particular was regularly emphasised within both survey contributions and teacher interviews. However, the interviews also revealed that teachers can find that restricted curriculum time and/or budgetary constraints limit the opportunities available to them. Certainly, this research study indicates that further analysis of the reasons behind the pedagogical, resource, and curriculum choices that teachers make would prove invaluable in the future development of Holocaust education programmes.

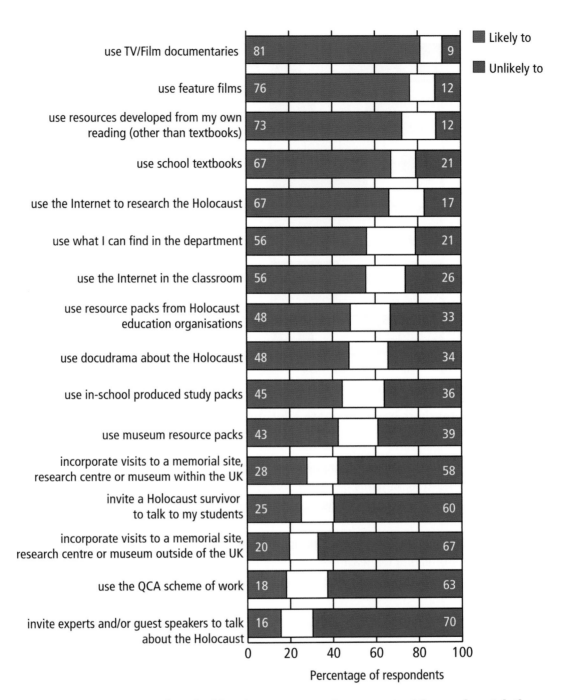

Figure 16: Survey question: 'Taking into account the opportunities and restrictions at my school, when teaching about the Holocaust I . . . '

HOW WELL SUPPORTED ARE TEACHERS IN TEACHING ABOUT THE HOLOCAUST?

Teachers were also invited to indicate along a five-point scale whether they 'never' (1) or 'always' (5) had adequate educational resources for teaching about the Holocaust. The responses of all teachers and citizenship, English, history and RE teachers are tabulated in Figure 17.

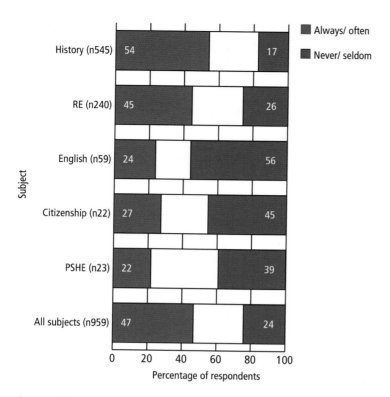

Figure 17: Do teachers have adequate educational resources for teaching about the Holocaust?

The results of the survey appear to suggest that, across subjects, history teachers believe they are the best provided for in terms of educational resources, especially compared to those who teach about the Holocaust within English, citizenship or PSHE.

As Figure 18 demonstrates, those who principally teach about the Holocaust within citizenship or English are also among the least likely to have received either initial teacher training (ITT), or in-service training (INSET)/continuing professional development (CPD) to help them do so.

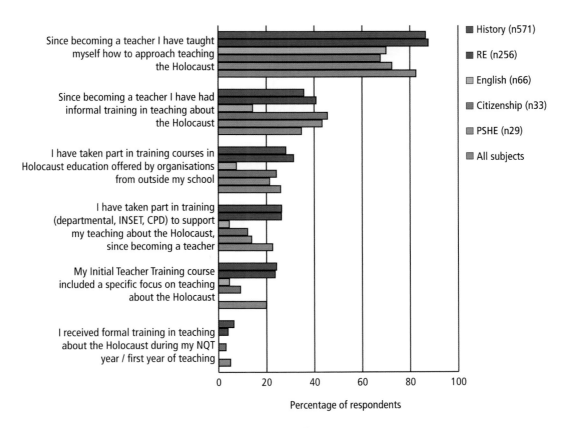

Percentage of respondents

Figure 18: Training received by survey respondents

While 13.8% of the PSHE teachers who taught about the Holocaust said they had received relevant INSET or CPD training, none had received any such training within their ITT course.

Figure 18 also shows that *all* teachers, irrespective of the subject in which they teach about the Holocaust, are most likely to consider themselves self-taught. Relatively few have received any form of formal training, whether through their initial teacher training provider, through INSET or CPD courses, or through organisations outside of their school.

Nonetheless, when asked to indicate how confident they felt in their knowledge and preparedness to teach about the Holocaust, as illustrated in Figures 19 and 20 most teachers in all subjects reported confidence.

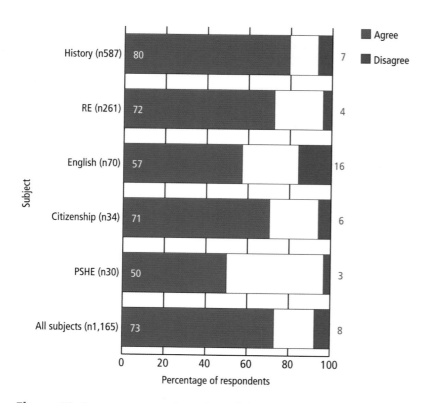

Figure 19: Survey respondents' confidence in their knowledge about the Holocaust

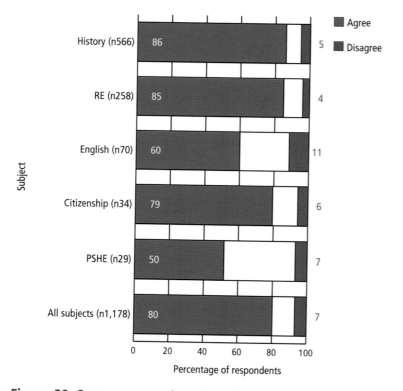

Figure 20: Survey respondents' confidence in their preparedness to teach about the Holocaust

TEACHERS' KNOWLEDGE OF THE HOLOCAUST

It was never the intention of this study to claim to be able to report on the overall level of knowledge about the Holocaust among teachers in English secondary schools. Without question, accurately and responsibly measuring 'knowledge levels' in *any* subject is an inherently complex and contentious task. However, teachers themselves stress the importance of accurate historical knowledge in teaching and learning about the Holocaust: as already reported, 87% (n917) of those who took part in the survey with teaching experience in this area agreed that they 'try to give students key facts and information about the Holocaust'. Nine 'knowledge-based' questions were included within the survey as it was considered important that the HEDP's research should be able to help identify any particular areas where teachers' knowledge may be better developed than in others. Furthermore, it was also deemed worthwhile to explore whether common misconceptions and misapprehensions about the Holocaust that are part of a general public discourse are feeding into representations of the past in the school classroom. This may be especially pertinent given the very low number of teachers who, according to this survey, have received any formal professional development in teaching about the Holocaust. Of these nine questions, six asked for a single response. Three further questions each had more than one correct answer, and teachers were invited to select a number of statements within each question. Teachers' responses to these nine questions are illustrated in the following charts. For each of the questions, analysis reveals how many teachers from each of the five principal subject areas gave each answer and considers and notes how many were correct.

Some tentative commentary is also possible to support the illustrative charts. For example, the first question listed below asked teachers when the 'systematic mass murder of Jewish people' began. Note that this question did not ask when Jewish people were first killed or when a plan to murder all of the Jewish people was decided upon. The consensus among academic historians (Bartov, 2000; Browning, 2004; Friedländer, 2007) is that while large numbers of Jewish people were killed prior to 1941, the mass murder became systematic only with *Einsatzgruppen* killings following the Nazi invasion of the Soviet Union, and a plan to murder all European Jews then developed some time after that. In total, 32.8% (n384) of survey respondents with experience of teaching about the Holocaust correctly answered, '1941, with the invasion of the Soviet Union'.

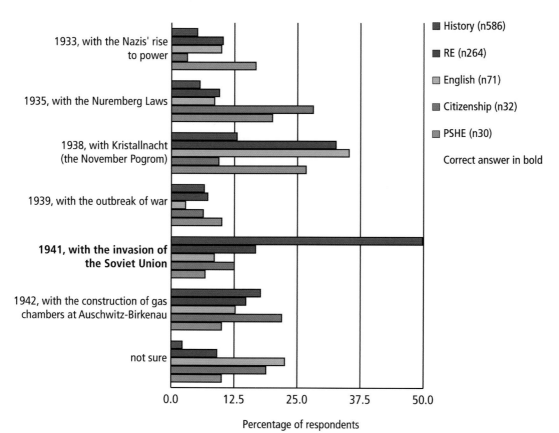

Figure 21: Survey question, 'Systematic mass murder of Jewish people began in . . .'

Yet, as Figure 21 illustrates, while almost 50% of history teachers gave this answer, both religious education and English teachers were more likely to locate the onset of systematic killing earlier, at 1938, with the November Pogrom (euphemistically known as *Kristallnacht* or the 'Night of Broken Glass') (32.6%, n86 and 35.2%, n25, respectively). Arguably, the notions of 'systematic' killing and 'mass murder' are both open to interpretation. However, it would be instructive to further examine why there appears to be a subject specific variation in understanding and/or perspective here.

A second question asked teachers, 'if a member of the German occupying forces refused an instruction to kill Jewish people, what would be the most likely consequence for that individual?' Although explored as a possible line of defence during the Nuremberg trials, no record has ever been found that a German soldier was killed or sent to a concentration camp for refusing such an order. Most historians today (Browning 1992; Friedlander 1998; Goldhagen 1996) suggest that the most likely consequence was that a soldier would be excused from the killing and given other duties.

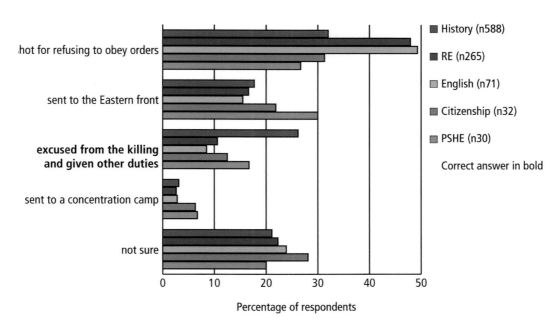

Figure 22: Survey question, 'If a member of the German occupying forces refused an instruction to kill Jewish people, the most likely outcome for that individual would be that they were . . .'

However, as shown in Figure 22, this does not appear to be the understanding held by many of the teachers who responded to the survey. This is perhaps an indication of the continuation in the school classroom of common misconceptions about the Holocaust that are prevalent in public discourse about the period. Arguably, this perception has potentially very important consequence for how teachers teach about the Holocaust and for students' understandings. The following chapter examines some of the aims that teachers articulate when teaching about the Holocaust and these include 'learning lessons from the past' and 'reflecting upon the choices and actions of individuals' who were involved in this historical event. Arguably, however, there are very different 'lessons to be learned' or understandings to be drawn if teachers believe that the Nazi perpetrators of violence and death faced a real risk to their lives if they did not carry out orders from above. There has been much academic research in recent years (Bankier, 1992; Browning, 1992; Cesarani, 2004) on explaining the motivations and actions of perpetrators, collaborators and bystanders in the Holocaust; the results of this survey may indicate that students in many English school classrooms are not currently being introduced to the key findings of this research.

A third knowledge-based question asked teachers to identify the first group to become victims of a Nazi mass murder programme (see Figure 23). This chronology is not a minor issue. It speaks to an understanding about the radicalisation of the Nazi policies of persecution and mass murder and to important relationships between the methods and personnel employed in the murder of different victim groups. The specific persecution of each victim group, the context in which salient Nazi policies and programmes developed, and the relationships between these programmes is essential to any understanding of this period.

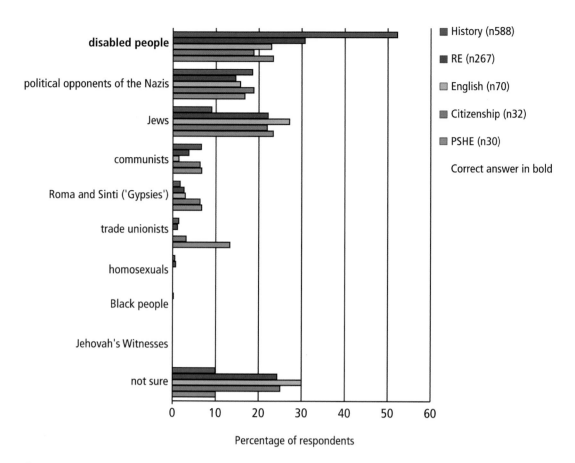

Figure 23: Survey question, 'The first group to become victims of a Nazi mass murder programme were . . .'

Arguably, therefore, as Figure 23 illustrates, it is interesting to note that many teachers correctly identified 'disabled people' as the first group to become victims of a Nazi mass murder programme. However, Chapter 4 describes in some detail that many teachers appear to consider it important that all Nazi victims should be recognised within the term 'the Holocaust'. On this basis one might anticipate that even more would be aware of the significance of the so-called 'Euthanasia' programme in marking the Nazis' radicalisation from policies of persecution to a full programme of mass murder. In this light, the number of teachers who answered this question incorrectly does raise some pertinent issues. For example, might it be that including all victims under the term 'Holocaust' is sometimes at the cost of careful and detailed consideration of why, how and in what ways each of these groups was actually persecuted? If so, what value does memory, or acknowledgement, of the diverse victim groups have without detailed understanding? And would there be more value in exploring the particular experiences, including the differences in persecution, of each victim group rather than universalising their experience under the umbrella term 'Holocaust'?

Another online survey question asked teachers to identify the origin of the country that provided the largest number of Jewish people murdered by the Nazis and their collaborators.

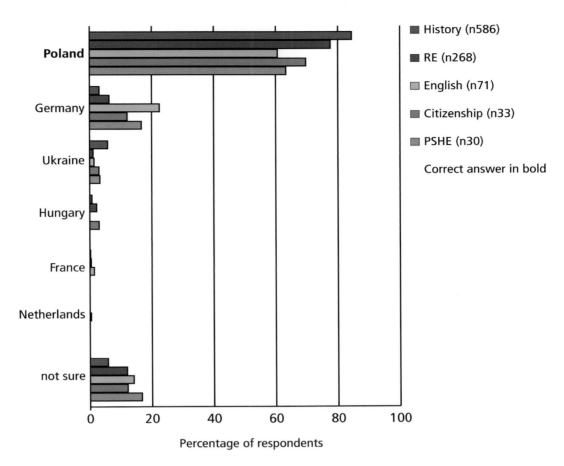

Figure 24: Survey question, 'The largest number of Jewish people murdered by the Nazis and their collaborators came from . . .'

As Figure 24 shows, large numbers of teachers in all five subject areas provided the correct answer (i.e., Poland). In particular, a high percentage of history teachers (84.5%, n495) and RE teachers (77.6%, n208) provided accurate responses, and this may be an indication of a good understanding of a dimension of the Holocaust that is not necessarily common knowledge.

A fifth knowledge-based question required teachers to best describe the British Government's policy towards Europe's Jews during the Second World War. The full responses offered to teachers are reproduced in Figure 25 below. 58.8% (n343) of history teachers and 50% (n15) of PSHE teachers provided the answer that best reflects recent research and the latest historiography (Kushner, 1994; London, 2003). In contrast, fewer than half of all English, RE and citizenship teachers who replied to the question answered in this way.

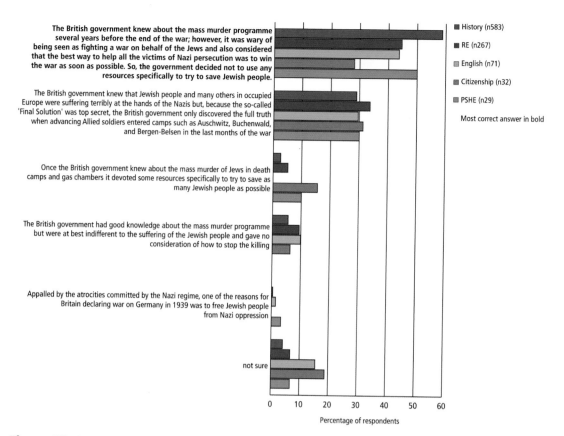

Figure 25: Survey question, 'Which of the following statements do you consider best describes the British Government's policy towards Europe's Jews during the Second World War?'

This question was included in the survey to get a sense of how the Holocaust is commonly incorporated into the British national narrative in English schools. The very low percentage of teachers from all subjects who believe that Britain declared war in 1939 in order to 'free Jewish people from Nazi oppression' is evidence that this particular national myth has very little currency in today's English school classroom. At the other extreme, few teachers also take the most condemnatory view of the wartime British Government – that despite having good knowledge about the mass murders of Jews they were 'at best indifferent to the suffering of the Jewish people and gave no consideration of how to stop the killing'.

A small but noteworthy number of citizenship teachers and a lower proportion of PSHE teachers mistakenly believe that the British Government dedicated resources specifically to rescue as many Jews as possible from the gas chambers, when in fact there was a conscious decision not to divert any resources from the war effort, and reluctance to treat the Jewish people's plight as being substantively different from the suffering of other people under German Nazi occupation. However, as the total number of both PSHE and citizenship teachers whose responses were captured is comparatively small, any implications drawn here must be very tentative indeed.

While it is accurate to say that the 'full' truth about the extent of the Holocaust only became clear after the liberation of the camps in the last months of the war, the relatively large number of teachers across all subjects who selected this as an explanation of British policy are perhaps over-influenced by the commonly-held misconception that the 'Final Solution' was a well-kept secret. It simply is not the case that the outside world did not know what was happening to the Jewish people until the end of the war. The continuation of this myth raises serious questions about what 'lessons' are being drawn from a study of the Holocaust in English schools, young people's understandings about the responsibility of the 'outside world' during the Holocaust, and the implications for the prevention of other genocides and mass atrocities in the world today.

The more convincing explanation of British policy – which recognises that there was early and accurate knowledge of the mass murder of Jews, but that no rescue plan was developed beyond winning the war as quickly as possible – was chosen by the largest numbers of teachers in all subject areas (except for citizenship). However, only among history teachers was this more than half of the respondents (58.8%, n343). Even among large numbers of history teachers (29%, n161) the misconception that the British Government did not have good knowledge about what was happening to the Jewish people until the end of the war appears to persist.

A sixth knowledge-based question asked teachers what, in percentage terms, was the Jewish population of Germany in 1933 (as illustrated in Figure 26).

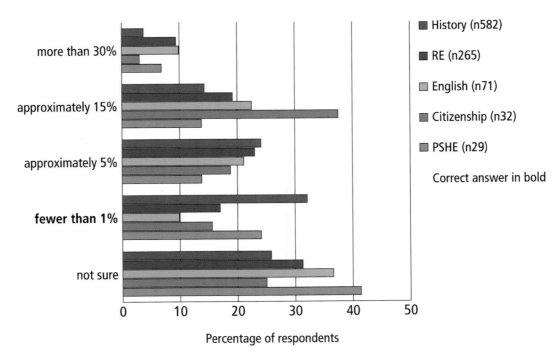

Figure 26: Survey question, 'In percentage terms, the Jewish population in Germany in 1933 was . . .'

Of note, the correct answer (i.e., fewer than 1%) was provided by a relatively small number of teachers in all subject areas, with less than one in five citizenship, English and RE teachers providing an accurate answer. Responses to the question also revealed a high degree of uncertainty among teachers in all subject areas.[18] Given that Nazi propaganda blamed the Jews for all the ills of the German nation and portrayed them as an existential threat to the survival of the German people, it is arguably very important that teachers and their students are aware of the very small numbers of Jews living in pre-war Germany. One of the unprecedented characteristics about the Holocaust, identified, for example, by Bauer (2001), is the anti-rational, anti-pragmatic nature of the Nazis' ideologically-driven programme that elevated a small, vulnerable minority group - that was loyal to the German nation and that made a wholly positive contribution to the German economy and society - to the level of deadly adversary that must be destroyed at all costs. If teachers commonly over-estimate the size of the German Jewish population by some 15 or 30 times, then it might be that myths and stereotypes about the power, wealth and control of this group are unwittingly reinforced. Once again, therefore, these varying levels of historical knowledge among teachers raise important questions about the ways in which the Holocaust is being taught about in English secondary schools.

A picture begins to emerge from the survey that many teachers appear to give relatively little attention to who the victims of the Holocaust actually were and how they responded to the persecution and genocide. The proportion of the German people who were Jewish is routinely over-estimated; relatively few teachers spend time covering the history and diversity of the Jewish people in Europe, pre-war Jewish life or the contribution that Jewish people made to the development of European society; nor do many focus on Jewish armed resistance to the Nazis in the camps or Jewish partisan activity (see also the discussion of topics covered in Chapter 4). It may be that this again reflects common representations of the Holocaust that have dominated in the decades following the Second World War and which have tended to reinforce a view of the Jewish people as a passive mass.

A further knowledge-based question asking teachers to identify some of the places of Jewish armed resistance allows for further detailed analysis of this issue, and the teachers' responses are shown in Figure 27.

---

[18] As determined by the percentage of teachers who indicated they were 'not sure' of the answer.

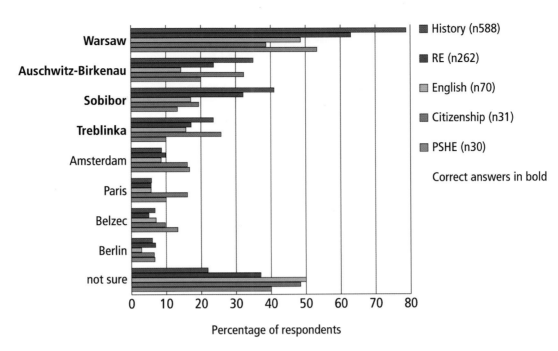

Figure 27: Survey question, 'Jewish armed revolts occurred in which of the following places?'

Another question asked teachers to identify killing centres constructed specifically for the task of murdering Jewish people (see Figure 28). Given the common assertion in public discourse that the details of the Holocaust are now widely known - even that more time and effort now should be spent on other subjects – and given also that only six death camps were constructed with the specific task to murder Jews within hours of their arrival, and that together these camps were responsible for the gassing of millions of men, women and children, it might be expected that teachers who teach about the Holocaust would be familiar with the names of these places.

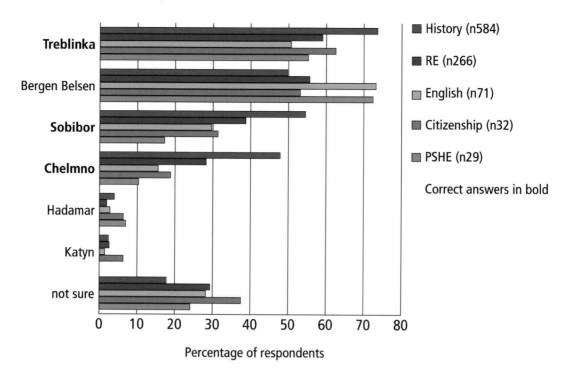

Figure 28: Survey question, 'Which of the following were killing centres built specifically for killing Jewish people?'

However, while very few teachers made the mistake of identifying Hadamar or Katyn as killing centres for the murder of Jews, much larger proportions of teachers from all subjects stated that they were unsure which sites were constructed specifically for this purpose. Furthermore, very high proportions of teachers in all subject areas mistakenly identified Bergen-Belsen as a death camp, perhaps because of the graphic images filmed there after liberation by the British army, the atrocities these images came to symbolise, and the powerful place that Bergen-Belsen has subsequently occupied in the British national narrative.

While Treblinka was correctly identified by 73.6% (n430) of history teachers and by high proportions of teachers in other subject areas, Sobibor was recognised by only a little more than half of history teachers (54.5%, n318) (and fewer still of teachers from other subjects), and Chelmno – the first death camp built for the murder of the Jewish people – was unknown to more than half of history teachers, to more than 70% of Religious Education teachers, and to more than 80% of teachers in all other subject areas. Of note, only 47.8% (n279) of history teachers, 28.2% (n75) of RE teachers, 15.5% (n11) of English teachers, 18.8% (n6), and 10.3% (n3) of PSHE teachers successfully identified Chelmno.

Interestingly, another aspect of this history – the November Pogrom, or *Kristallnacht* – appears to be much better-known amongst teachers of the Holocaust, and many were able to correctly answer some detailed questions about this night of violence, as shown in Figure 29, below.

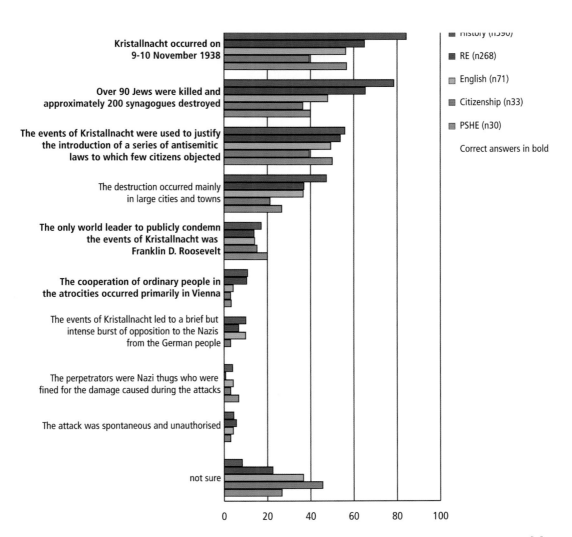

Figure 29: Survey question, 'Which of the following statements are accurate with regard to Kristallnacht?'

It may be that many teachers in England are more familiar with the Nazi period up to the outbreak of the Second World War than they are with the development of the Holocaust during the period 1939-45.

As previously stated, it would not be prudent to draw sweeping conclusions about levels of teachers' knowledge from the data presented here. Undoubtedly, this is an area of research that warrants more detailed analysis and investigation. Nevertheless, this brief snapshot of teachers' knowledge about the Holocaust suggests a number of important gaps and, potentially, misunderstandings. While the results of this early exploration must not be overplayed, they do not appear to support the very high levels of confidence that many teachers indicate in their self-assessment of their knowledge about this complex historical subject. At this stage, however, it is only possible to speculate on the reasons for this apparent disparity:

- A strong record of teaching in English schools about the history of both Nazi Germany and the Second World War exists and it is likely that many teachers have considerable and detailed knowledge about these important areas. It may be that the Holocaust is seen by some teachers from within these important contextual frameworks and this could account for their high levels of confidence. However, the Holocaust has been the subject of intense and detailed academic research in its own right, and some teachers might not have had the opportunity to update their substantive knowledge in this specific, complex history.

- The Holocaust has, over the last 15 years or so, become ever more present in the collective memory of the British people, with many and diverse representations in popular culture, film and media. Familiarity with these popular narratives and representations of the Holocaust might give teachers confidence in their knowledge of this past while at the same time perpetuating certain popular myths, misconceptions and misapprehensions about the Holocaust.

- Certainties and sincerely held notions about the meaning of the Holocaust, its importance and the lessons it holds – which are clearly indicated by other elements of the research – might lead to over-estimations about one's historical knowledge. The meaning and 'lessons' might seem so stark, so clear, that teachers could feel confident that they are well equipped to convey these messages to their students, while not necessarily having desirable levels of detailed historical knowledge.

Above all, this brief snapshot of teachers' knowledge tentatively suggests that teaching in all subject areas could significantly benefit from CPD programmes that provide teachers with the essential historical knowledge required to teach about the Holocaust in meaningful ways.

SUMMARY

The primary purpose of Chapter 3 was to provide a systematic empirical overview of key patterns and trends in Holocaust education in English secondary schools. Drawing primarily on an analysis of survey data, it provided a wealth of information on a range of issues including the numbers of teachers teaching about the Holocaust in a variety of subject areas, the amount of curriculum time devoted to the subject, the training that teachers receive, the topics they teach and the resources most frequently used. The chapter also reported on teachers' levels of knowledge and their preparedness and confidence to teach about the Holocaust. Importantly, analysis of the data revealed a number of significant issues vital to any understanding of Holocaust education in England and to the development of CPD programmes for teachers. For example, it exposed the issue of the limited amount of curriculum time devoted to the Holocaust in some subject areas and across different year groups. It also raised numerous questions and concerns both about the status and nature of teachers' topic choices and the adequacy of teacher knowledge when teaching about the Holocaust. Chapter 4 explores some of these issues in more detail. Indeed, whereas Chapter 3 provided a comprehensive outline of key trends in English secondary schools in terms of teaching about the Holocaust, Chapter 4 provides a more detailed analysis of the rationale that underpins teachers' pedagogical and curriculum choices.

You kind of just assume to some extent that they *should* know about the Holocaust, rather than even think about whether there's any reason *why* they should know about it.

History teacher, North West, emphasis added

CHAPTER 4: TEACHERS' AIMS AND UNDERSTANDINGS WHEN APPROACHING THE HOLOCAUST

INTRODUCTION

While Chapter 3 presented an overview of generalised trends in teaching about the Holocaust across England, Chapter 4 is concerned with the perspectives of individual teachers. More specifically, the reasons why teachers make certain decisions and/or adopt particular teaching approaches are explored. Key questions under consideration include: what exactly do teachers understand by the term, 'the Holocaust?' What informs an individual teacher's understanding? Are teachers clear as to *why* they teach about the Holocaust? Do they have specific and/or clearly articulated teaching aims? How do teachers' aims relate to their understandings? And what is the significance of the subject area in which their teaching about the Holocaust takes place?

HOW DO TEACHERS UNDERSTAND OR DEFINE THE HOLOCAUST?

In a 2006 study, *Teaching the Holocaust in School History,* former secondary school history teacher Lucy Russell argued that there was 'a lack of consensus regarding the basic assumptions' underpinning teaching in this area, such as what the term, 'the Holocaust' even means (2006: 45). Teachers' understandings and definitions therefore comprised an important dimension both of the survey and of follow-up interview-based research.

An early question within the online survey acknowledged that 'many different understandings of the Holocaust exist' but then required teachers to choose, from the following list of seven suggestions, the one statement that most closely matched their own:

A. The Holocaust was the persecution and murder of a range of victims perpetrated by the Nazi regime and its collaborators. They were targeted for different reasons and were persecuted in different ways. Victims included Jews, Gypsies, disabled people, Poles, Slavs, homosexuals, Jehovah's Witnesses, Soviet prisoners or war, Black people, and other political and ethnic groups.

B. The Nazis and their collaborators perpetrated crimes against humanity on millions of people. The Holocaust was the attempt to murder every last Jewish person in Europe. Other groups were targeted for destruction but, unlike the Jews, there was no plan to murder every member of these other groups.

C. The Holocaust was the systematic, bureaucratic, state-sponsored persecution and murder of approximately six million Jews by the Nazi regime and its collaborators.

D. Hitler believed that ethnic Germans were the members of a 'Master Race'. For the sake of their 'new order', which would see this 'Master Race' dominate the continent of Europe, the Nazis attempted to get rid of anyone who was 'different' from them and this resulted in the mass murder of millions of people: we call this the Holocaust.

E. The persecution of Jewish people during the Second World War, which is often referred to as 'the Holocaust' has been exaggerated. The figure of six million killed is too high. While there is no doubt that many Jewish people died during this time, this was in the context of a world war where some 50 million people are believed to have been killed.

F. The Holocaust has a universal meaning to describe unspeakable suffering, persecution and atrocity.

G. The Holocaust is used in so many different ways, by different groups and individuals for different purposes that it has lost any specific and agreed meaning.

The list had been compiled to reflect the concerns of Russell (*ibid.*), Salmons (2003) and others that significant differences and contradictions exist between historians' definitions and popular understandings of the term. Specifically, the survey question was designed to examine respondents' perspectives on two key areas of contention:

1. Whether or not 'the Holocaust' should refer to a specific, radical form of genocide perpetrated against the Jews of Nazi-occupied Europe or whether it should also be used with reference to other groups persecuted by the Nazi regime.

2. Whether or not 'the Holocaust' should refer specifically to the experience of the Jewish population of Nazi-occupied Europe, or whether it should also be used with reference to other groups persecuted and targeted by the Nazi regime.

Respondents were also given the opportunity to reject all seven of these suggestions and to offer instead their own understanding of the term.

Among the total 2,108 individuals who completed the survey, 1,976 responded and their answers are illustrated in Figure 30.

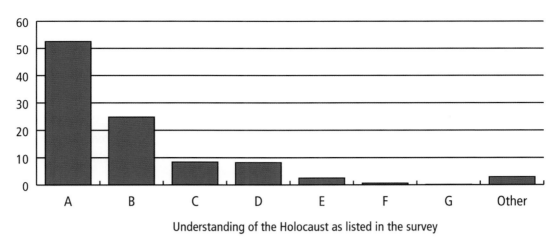

Figure 30: Survey respondents' understandings of the Holocaust (n1,976)

52.5% (n1,038) of all respondents chose statement A, which locates the Holocaust within the Nazi period and includes all victims of Nazi persecution without specifying any substantive differences in Nazi policy towards these groups. Statement B also recognises that other groups were targeted for destruction but specifies that the policy towards the Jews was substantively different because, 'unlike the Jews, there was no plan to murder *every member* of these other groups' (emphasis added). This was the second most popular option, but was chosen by less than half the number of teachers who chose statement A (24.8%, n490, of all respondents). Statements C, which references only the Nazi persecution and murder of Jews and does not indicate what was particular about this policy, and D, which more broadly references the Nazis' attempt 'to get rid of anyone who was "different"', were chosen by 8.2% (n163) and 8.4% (n165) respectively. The broadest understandings – reflected in statements F and G - which do not locate the Holocaust specifically within Nazi-occupied Europe and either universalise its meaning or deny it any specific meaning at all – were chosen by only 2.5% (n49) and 0.6% (n11) of all respondents. Only two individuals who completed the survey chose statement E.

In total, 58 respondents chose to contribute their own understanding of what the term 'the Holocaust' means. Examination of these free-text responses reveals that, in many cases, teachers wanted to slightly reword or, more commonly, combine two or more of the suggestions provided in the survey. Frequently this represented an individual's attempt to find their own balance between recognising *both* the specificity of Jewish experience *and* the victimisation and targeting of other groups.

Other free-text responses indicated that their authors wanted, among other things, to:

- problematise the extent to which the Holocaust was 'necessarily *completely* systematic in its application' as suggested by statement C (emphasis added)

- recognise that competing understandings of the Holocaust currently circulate

- draw attention to the roles performed by ordinary people and not just Nazi rulers

- make some attempt at indicating the *causes* of the Holocaust, for example:

> The Holocaust was the result of Nazi ideology which under the influence of cumulative radicalism, imperial ambition and the pressures of war drove German society to the purging of those considered undesirable.
>
> Extract from survey response

While one respondent directly challenged the relevance of choosing between the different understandings listed ('These are overlapping descriptions and trying to differentiate between them is largely a meaningless exercise in semantics') others argued that the clarity and utility of the term was increasingly under threat:

> The term 'the holocaust' [sic] refers specifically to the systematic annihilation of the Jews (point [C]), but is commonly used as an umbrella term to include the persecution of other groups (point [A]). In this sense, I would suggest that the term is becoming more a generic term, almost synonymous with genocide. A redefinition and specificity is required.
>
> Extract from survey response

This respondent articulated a central concern of a number of Holocaust historians and educators in this field (Bauer 2001; Russell 2006; Salmons 2001). In terms of defining 'the Holocaust', the general consensus among academic historians - as suggested by the Taskforce for International Cooperation on Holocaust Education, Remembrance and Research - is most closely reflected in statements B and, to a lesser extent, statement C from the survey list (for a fuller discussion see the ITF Education Working Group's *Guidelines for Teaching* (2004). Far from being 'an exercise in meaningless semantics', commentators such as Salmons and Russell (*op cit.*) consider that a teacher's understanding or definition of the Holocaust can have profound pedagogical consequence.

(WHY) DO DEFINITIONS MATTER?

When asked during the survey, 51% (n529) of all respondents who have taught or currently teach about the Holocaust said they agreed or strongly agreed that, 'The Holocaust is clearly very important but so are other genocides and crimes against humanity: these should get similar curriculum time and attention'. Fewer than 17% (n173) of all those with experience of teaching in this area disagreed with this position. This raises an important question articulated in some of the free-text responses given by teachers completing the survey: why is the Holocaust singled out as a compulsory component of the National Curriculum? What is its specific historical and/or other educational significance?

Echoing the results of the survey, few teachers who were interviewed considered that it was appropriate to use the term 'the Holocaust' with application outside of the persecutions of Nazi Europe. However, and as will be discussed in further detail below, several believed it important to draw attention in their teaching to what they considered were comparable situations elsewhere in the world, for example in Rwanda, Bosnia Herzegovina and Darfur. Where teachers made the case that the Holocaust *was* important to distinguish from such other genocides, most made reference to its scale or to the systematic and/or industrialised nature of the Nazi killing rather than to the unprecedented totality of the Nazi intention to murder *every* Jewish person *everywhere*.

During interviews, teachers were asked directly whether they thought that 'the Holocaust' referred *only* to the targeting of Jews or could – or *should* – encompass other persecuted groups. Among those who did suggest that it was important to make a distinction, their rationale was often explained with reference to the roots of the word itself, or was related to a sense of the relative 'scale of suffering' of different groups:

> Well, I find it quite difficult, because again it's coming from the Jewish perspective, and the word 'Holocaust' derives from the Jewish tradition.[19] So in that sense, 'Holocaust', I guess, should refer to the Jewish people. I think it does a disservice to the other groups of people that were persecuted, if we only focus on the Jews. So therefore I wouldn't necessarily use the term 'Holocaust' when I was talking about the other groups that were persecuted but I wouldn't teach the Holocaust and the persecution of the Jews in isolation from the other things that were going on at the time.
>
> RE teacher, South West

> Well, I certainly put it into some kind of relative concept that certainly the Jews suffered by far . . . the most, but that's not to say that there was not other people involved.
>
> History teacher, North West

Although some teachers drew attention to the fact that different groups were targeted by the Nazis for different reasons, the distinction that it was only the Jewish population who were targeted for complete annihilation within Europe was raised by very few teachers in interview.[20] Yet it is on the basis of precisely this distinction – that the Holocaust represents the first time in history that every member of an *entire* population were targeted for complete extermination *across* national boundaries and on purely ideological, putatively 'racial', grounds – that the Holocaust historian Yehuda Bauer (2001) argues that the Holocaust is an 'unprecedented' historical event.

From this perspective, it is of potential concern that the majority of all teachers who completed the online survey chose a statement of understanding which *does not* seem to reflect current

---

[19] In fact the word 'Holocaust' is of Greek origin.

[20] One teacher offered almost this argument and allied the experience and position of the Roma people alongside that of the Jews:

> I mean, the one other group of people then, that does need to be included, are the Romani people, because that is a clear parallel: there was a specific, programme of extermination. And it might, in some respects, seem a slightly marginal difference, like yes, but there is a difference between the Third Reich's policy as it developed from forty-one onwards, between the Jewish people and the Romani people, and the savage persecution of other groups of people, but that was not actually a programme of extermination.
>
> History teacher, West Midlands.

It is also worth noting here that the Nazi genocide of the Roma is still a matter of ongoing academic debate and the subject of continuing historical research.

academic research on this history and does not recognise the specificity of the Nazis' targeting of European Jews.

INFLUENCES ON TEACHERS' UNDERSTANDINGS OF THE HOLOCAUST

By combining analysis of the survey data and follow-up interviews a number of influences on teachers' understandings of the Holocaust are identified, explored and outlined below.

Subject background and prior teaching experience in this area

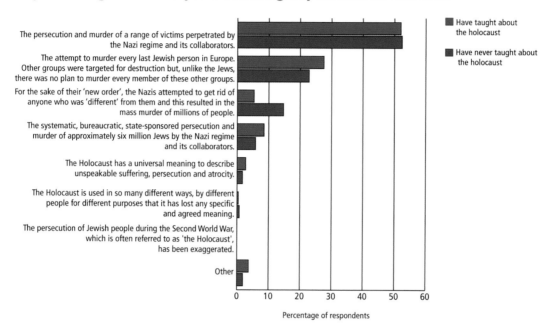

Figure 31: Survey respondents' understandings of the Holocaust by prior teaching experience

The dominance of statement A ('The Holocaust was the persecution and murder of a range of victims perpetrated by the Nazi regime and its collaborators') remained consistent irrespective of whether or not respondents had any prior experience of teaching about the Holocaust: it was chosen by 52% of those with such experience (n612) and 52.4% of those without (n306). It was also the most popular statement of understanding across all five subjects in which teaching about the Holocaust principally takes place: it was chosen by 64.7% (n22) of citizenship teachers, 60% (n18) of PSHE teachers, 52.9% (n311) of history teachers, 49.3% (n132) of RE teachers. Further detail of the responses given by each of these groups of teachers is illustrated in Figure 31 and Figure 32.

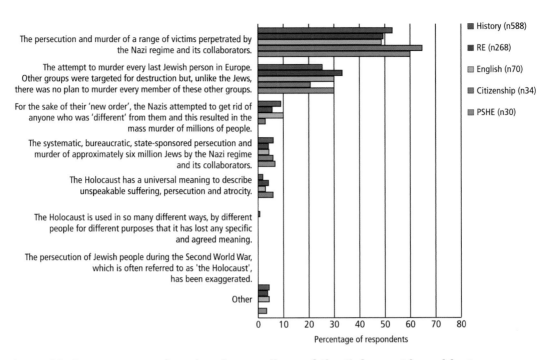

Figure 32: Survey respondents' understandings of the Holocaust by subject

Knowledge

Although this is an area that would benefit from further detailed investigation, by using the responses given to the knowledge-based questions described in the previous chapter, it is also possible to explore, albeit tentatively, the relationship between an individual teacher's historical knowledge of the events of the Holocaust and their understanding of the term. Data from the online survey would appear to suggest that a teacher's knowledge has more of an impact on how they understand the term 'the Holocaust' than either their subject background or their prior experience of teaching in this area (although it is also important to acknowledge that there is likely to be an interdependent relationship between the three).

Of the nine knowledge-based survey questions that respondents were asked, six had only one correct answer. Among all respondents, 48 teachers answered all six of these questions correctly while 305 did not correctly answer any at all. Figure 33 illustrates the relationship between the number of questions an individual correctly answered and the understanding that they chose.

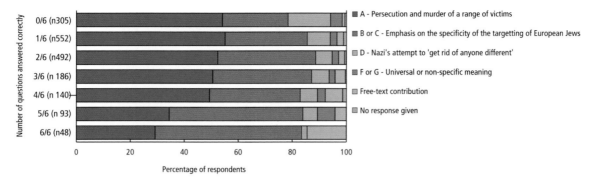

Figure 33: Variation in understandings of the Holocaust by accuracy of survey respondents' 'knowledge base'[21]

Figure 33 suggests that the more 'knowledgeable' a teacher responding to the survey appears to be (on the basis of the answers given to these six knowledge questions), the more likely they are to reject statement A in favour of an understanding which recognises the specificity of the targeting of European Jews (i.e., either statement B or C from the list above).[22] The same teachers also appear far less likely to choose statement D, which describes the Nazis' attempt to 'get rid of anyone who is "different"' in the most general terms.

Voices of authority

Follow-up interviews provided an important opportunity to further examine the origin of individual teachers' understandings. When asked to offer their own personal definition of 'the Holocaust' a number of the teachers who were interviewed made immediate reference to the significance of something that they had learned, heard or read elsewhere. For example, a number of teachers problematised the term 'Holocaust' (meaning "whole burnt offering") suggesting alternatives such as 'Shoah' (meaning 'catastrophe') and/or 'Churban' (meaning 'destruction'). On more than one occasion this was explained explicitly with reference to the fact that:

> Well, in one of the textbooks it says that, the Holocaust isn't perhaps the best word to use and in fact, is it 'Churban' or something isn't it? [I]n the *Peace and War* textbook it's like the opening statement almost.

> Head of history, North East

Other teachers explained that they had learned from 'members of the Jewish community' that these alternatives were more appropriate to use. [23]

Many teachers also demonstrated that they wanted to be reflexive in their understandings and that their definitions were open to revision or change in light of books read, museums visited, discussions with Holocaust survivors or encounters with specialist educators in this field. Interestingly, several of those teachers who described a change in their definition of the Holocaust suggested that they were now *more* likely than in the past to use the term with

---

[21] Here 'knowledge base' is tentatively indicated by the answers given to six survey questions, that each had only one correct answer.

[22] None of the teachers who provided any answers at all for these knowledge-based questions chose understanding E, the statement reflecting the position of Holocaust deniers.

[23] For an academic discussion of alternative terms for the Holocaust, see Landau (1992).

reference to the variety of non-Jewish groups targeted by the Nazis. For example, one young teacher described that his recent PGCE training had drawn attention to the Nazi persecution of groups like the Roma and the experiences of homosexuals. He believed that the point his trainers were making was that teachers should 'not lose sight of those other groups' and so revised his definition accordingly.[24] Similarly, the focus of activity around recent commemorations to mark Holocaust Memorial Day was also cited by some teachers as a reason to,

> start thinking about other holocausts and other genocides, whereas before then, I probably . . . only did think about the Second World War.
>
> History and sociology teacher, South East

Instrumental Definitions

A number of teachers made a distinction between *their own* definition or understanding and the sort of definition that they would choose to use with students in their schools.

In some cases, teachers indicated that the definitions they offered students would be simplified. For example, one teacher began by saying that he recognised there was a great deal of complexity and debate surrounding the term and that sometimes he would discuss this with his students, although it would depend on the 'sort of ability range' of his class:

> Lower ability I think it just hopelessly confuses them whereas it's better to just give them a straightforward definition as such.
>
> History teacher, South West

Other teachers remarked that the GCSE or A level syllabus and/or particular schemes of work in earlier school years also impacted upon the definitions that they used. One group of teachers noted that, at GCSE, they were more likely than with younger students to emphasise a variety of victim groups within their definition of the Holocaust. This was because:

> the way the syllabus is, it only goes up to 1941 doesn't it? So it really applies to sort of the early days of Nazi Germany in which case, what you do is you do sort of talk about *all* the groups rather than the 'Final [Solution]'. You don't really talk about the 'Final Solution', because it's not on the syllabus.
>
> History teacher, North East

Elsewhere teachers argued that making their definition 'relevant' to students was key. For example, 'relevance' was invoked as an argument for taking care *not* to emphasise only the Jewish experience in Nazi Germany:

> **Teacher A**: One of the ways that you can make it relevant to the pupils, because we're in a multi-racial school, is the fact that anybody who is of a different race, who is not of the 'Aryan' race, would not be living here if the Nazis had actually won the war.
>
> **Teacher B**: I think that's really relevant in a school like this, isn't it? Where we've got such a high number of Asian kids.

---

[24] In fact, the organisation that delivered this teacher's training does not share his inclusive definition of the Holocaust. 'Voices of authority' are not necessarily heard or interpreted in the manner intended.

Teacher C: Yes, so we try and look at it in a much broader way than just the Jews.

Geography and history teachers, West Midlands

Another teacher believed his students became especially interested when he highlighted that disabled people were among the victims of the Nazi regime. He suggested that this was because most of the students he taught had little contact with Jewish people whereas discussion of those with a disability had more immediate resonance.

'Relevance' was also used as an argument by some teachers for broadening the definition of the term 'Holocaust' to include more recent, world events:

> To make it relevant to the students, I would always try using the Santayana thing, those who forget history and so forth. I would always try and bring the reference to the events in Bosnia and Rwanda and so forth, so students can see that it has a relevance for them.

History teacher, North East

Teachers in a school with a large number of students who were themselves refugees from war-torn countries also emphasised the importance of relating the Holocaust to current events. These teachers added that the Holocaust could mean 'different things to different people' depending on their own personal experience.

Some teachers were very explicit in linking their definitions to particular teaching aims. For example, one teacher – who had made a point of adding reference to the experience of non-Jewish targeted groups when her colleague offered a narrower definition of the Holocaust – explained:

> I suppose one of the reasons I've partly put the, if you like the 'P.S.' in, of 'others too', is in connection with, 'can it happen again?' – does it happen again? – in the 'lessons' side of it, to realise that the idea of difference is a key component.

History teacher, North East

In a similar manner, in a contribution to the online survey, another teacher made a deliberate point to highlight that, 'the indifference of many Germans and Austrians to the persecution and fate of Jews and other minority groups was a significant factor in the nature of the Holocaust'. She believed this indifference was 'relevant to today if there are lessons to be learned'.

WHAT ARE TEACHERS' AIMS WHEN TEACHING ABOUT THE HOLOCAUST?

In fact, the question of whether there are 'lessons to be learned' from the Holocaust is another key area of interest and debate. The overwhelming majority of survey respondents who taught (or had taught) about the Holocaust agreed or strongly agreed with the statement, 'I think it will always be important to teach about the Holocaust'. This was irrespective of their subject background. Across all teachers 94% (n1,002) of respondents agreed with this statement varying from 93.8% (n30) of citizenship teachers to 95.4% (n550) of those teaching about the

Holocaust in history. Large numbers also agreed that they thought 'it is right that teaching about the Holocaust is compulsory in the history school curriculum' (85.1%, n887 of all those with experience teaching in this area). More than half agreed that 'teaching about the Holocaust should be compulsory in one or more other subject areas' (62.2%, n644).

However, follow-up interviews suggested that teachers are not always entirely sure why this should be so:

> It's an interesting one that you should ask that, because it's something really, you kind of just assume to some extent that they should know about the Holocaust, rather than even think about whether there's any reason why they should know about it.
>
> History teacher, North East

At another school, one teacher emphasised the enormous significance that she placed on the subject:

> I always say to them [her students] if you never ever remember anything else that we are teaching you in this classroom – in this school – I want you to learn the lesson we are teaching you today.
>
> History and integrated humanities teacher, East Midlands

But what exactly is the 'lesson' she hoped her students would learn? If there are 'lessons to be learned' from the Holocaust, what are they? And how might they be best approached within school?

The teacher above explained further that, from her perspective, the important lesson is:

> [t]o know there is no such thing as a superior human being. And there is no such thing as being able to treat other people in a way that is different from the way you would want yourself to be treated.

Existing research in this area has suggested that across the UK and further afield, many teachers approaching the Holocaust work with similarly ambitious, broadly social and/or moral aims (see for example, Hector 2000; Russell 2006; Supple 1992). However, this represents yet another contentious area: other teachers, and many academic commentators, are sceptical as to whether these are appropriate or feasible teaching aims (see for example, Kinloch 1998). More specifically, some suggest that teachers working within different subject areas should approach the study of the Holocaust with distinct disciplinary aims.

In two recent issues of the Historical Association's teaching journal, *Teaching History*, a number of authors addressed issues related to 'historical', 'social' and/or 'moral' aims (2001; 2007a). Elsewhere within the academic discipline of history, some theorists and researchers warn against 'practical', or 'present oriented', instrumental uses of the past (see for example, Lee 1984, 1991; Lee, et al., 1992; Tosh 2008). From these perspectives, the past informs and shapes the present and the future in more subtle and complex ways than the notion of identifiable and neatly packaged 'lessons from the past' suggests. As highlighted in Chapter 1, it would be inaccurate to suggest that in England a single coherent set of aims and purposes for school history exists. While it is not the purpose of this report to examine the nature of school history in detail here, these contextual arguments are salient in interpreting both the survey data and interview-based teachers' accounts.

The online survey attempted to explore such issues by asking respondents to reflect on their own specific teaching aims. Teachers were presented with the following list of 13 suggestions and instructed to indicate the three that most closely matched the aims they considered especially important when teaching about the Holocaust:

A. to develop an understanding of the roots and ramifications of prejudice, racism, and stereotyping in any society

B. to reflect upon the theological questions raised by events of the Holocaust

C. to reflect upon the moral and/or ethical questions raised by events of the Holocaust

D. to reflect upon political questions, about power and/or abuse of power, raised by events of the Holocaust

E. to explore the roles and responsibilities of individuals, organisations, and governments when confronted with human rights' violations and/or policies of genocide

F. to deepen knowledge of World War II and Twentieth Century history

G. to preserve the memory of those who suffered

H. to understand and explain the actions of people involved in and affected by an unprecedented historical event

I. to explore questions about the foundations of Western civilisation

J. to explore the implications of remaining silent and indifferent in the face of the oppression of others

K. to learn the lessons of the Holocaust and to ensure that a similar human atrocity never happens again.

Across all survey respondents, 'to develop an understanding of the roots and ramifications of prejudice, racism and stereotyping in any society' was the most popularly prioritised teaching aim, chosen by 71% (n1,397). This was followed by, 'to learn the lessons of the Holocaust and to ensure that a similar human atrocity never happens again', chosen by 55.9% (n1,091). The popularity of these two teaching aims was consistent irrespective of whether or not teachers had prior experience teaching in this area.

ARE THERE SUBJECT SPECIFIC AIMS FOR TEACHING ABOUT THE HOLOCAUST?

The same two teaching aims also remained dominant irrespective of teachers' subject background (see Figure 34).

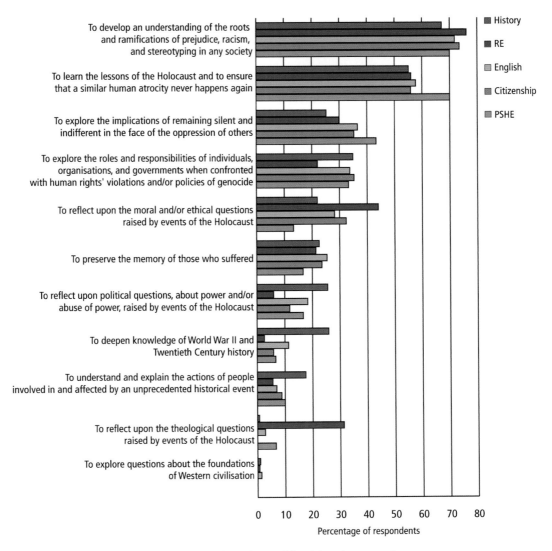

Figure 34: Variation in teachers' aims by subject background

However, the survey data suggested greater subject-based variation existed among those teachers who prioritised some of the other listed teaching aims. For example, aims B and C - 'to reflect upon the theological questions raised by the events of the Holocaust' and 'to reflect upon the moral and/or ethical questions raised by the events of the Holocaust' – were proportionately most popular among teachers of RE. Aims D, F and H - 'to reflect upon political questions about power and/or abuse of power', 'to deepen knowledge of World War II and Twentieth Century history' and 'to understand and explain the actions of people involved in and affected by an unprecedented historical event' - were more popular among teachers of history. However, only half as many history teachers prioritised each of these three options as chose option A or K.

This data would appear to indicate that distinct disciplinary objectives are less likely to be prioritised by teachers than overarching aims which cut across subject boundaries and disciplines. In certain respects this was also borne out in interview. In some of the schools visited, history teachers were joined by colleagues from other departments and in all interviews teachers were asked if they knew of other teaching about the Holocaust taking place elsewhere within their schools. These discussions provided an interesting opportunity for teachers to reflect on what was distinctive about a historical approach to teaching about the Holocaust – or a religious education, or citizenship approach as the case may be. Although, very broadly, religious education specialists were the teachers most likely to emphasise theological dimensions - such as discussion of the nature of evil, for example – and history teachers were the most likely to refer to the acquisition of skills such as 'source evaluation' and/or 'working with chronologies', there was little consistency across teachers' answers. One teacher who taught in both subjects explicitly remarked that it would not make any difference to her teaching aims whether she was delivering lessons on the Holocaust within history or within RE. Teachers were also asked why they thought that the Holocaust was a compulsory part of specifically the history curriculum. While some teachers answered that they felt an accurate historical knowledge of the period was fundamentally important to understanding the Holocaust and its context, others found this a difficult question to answer and were unclear.

FURTHER EXPLORATION

Unpacking the notion of distinct teaching aims is a complex endeavour and more detailed exploration is necessary here. The survey once again gave respondents the opportunity to offer their own additional thoughts and reflections on the question of teaching aims. Of the 88 responses recorded, several noted the difficulty entailed in choosing only three aims: indeed, a number of teachers remarked that all 13 of those that were listed informed their teaching in some way.

Some teachers also suggested that their teaching aims would vary, 'dependent on the context in which [the Holocaust] is taught'. Sometimes this variation was described in response to the nature of the lesson:

> In a lesson looking at suffering and belief in God I would have different aims than in a lesson looking at prejudice etc.

And sometimes in response to the students that were being taught:

> Depending on the attention span of students in any school, some of the above, particularly the intense political studies, may be too in depth for secondary schools.

Extracts from survey responses

Other teachers highlighted aims that they believed had not been captured by those suggested within the survey such as:

- 'to challenge Holocaust denial'

- 'to consider the resulting philosophical questions about the value of life. The nature and purpose of evil and the psychological effects of the atrocities on individuals'

- 'to maintain the emotional response of horror to the crimes of the Holocaust by retelling individual stories, e.g. *Schindler's List*.

Extracts from survey responses

Some teachers also gave greater insight into their own perspectives on subject specific teaching aims. For example, one respondent chose to prioritise: understanding the roots and ramifications of racism and prejudice; exploring the roles and responsibilities of individuals, organisations, and governments when confronted with human rights violations; and, exploring the implications of remaining silent and indifferent in the face of the oppression of others, but then used the free-text opportunity to add, 'this has to come from detailed historical study. It cannot be done in abstract'. Another respondent took a rather different perspective rejecting all 13 suggested aims and arguing:

> My problem with the above aims is that they are using History for other purposes, which I believe to be an abuse. I would argue that the Holocaust should be taught in itself as one of the more significant events in C20, and that young people should expect to know about it and draw their own conclusions - including that the Holocaust is not alone as such an atrocity, albeit probably the most systematic version of it.
>
> Extract from survey response

A similar tension was apparent within interviews, as is illustrated in the two extended extracts presented below:

> Well I think what I'm trying to do, is to get the pupils to understand the events as they happened chronologically, the reasons why they happened, the consequences of the actions of the individuals involved . . . I mean, I guess those are the key things, aren't they? The reasons why; the consequences of those actions.
>
> So in one sense it's like any other topic, if you like . . . from sort of a history point of view. And obviously you could compare events with other events but I think also . . . like the historical . . . getting them sort of to try to, to empathise to some extent with the situation of those people who were involved is really important and a valuable part of that process as well . . .
>
> I've got to be honest, I mean, the historical side of it is important, don't get me wrong, but it's kind of like almost to the . . . It's just *there*, do you know what I mean? And when I'm teaching it, the moral significance of it – the human significance of it – is far more prevalent for me personally.
>
> And I'd be kind of worried if there were people there who were just really interested in the chronology. And if I came out of my lesson thinking that pupils in the class just thought of it as just another topic, I would be a bit disappointed. In fact I wouldn't just be disappointed, I'd be really upset.
>
> History teacher, North West

> I mean, in very simple terms, why *I* think it's important - what *my* aim really is - is for the students to understand and appreciate how this is a significant event in history. And they must understand that it is a significant event and why it is so. I mean you can look at other events and say why they are significant, as well. Now this might sound a little bit cold, and I think it does, you know, to say, oh, all right, I'm just treating it in a sense like another event. A very important one, but another one. But . . . I don't think it's my job to sort of tell them the morality of this. It is for them to work it out . . . The way I approach it is in a very sort of straightforward way. I

mean, you have to look at the context. You have to look at why it took place at that particular time and you also have to say what happened.

History teacher, East Midlands

Although the first history teacher begins describing his own teaching aims with an emphasis on 'chronological' and other historical skills, he remarks that he would be 'really upset' if students left his classroom thinking of the Holocaust as 'just another topic'. When asked what he would want his students to have achieved at the end of a unit of work on the Holocaust, he replied,

> I'd want some sort of moral development, you know? What's the point in having like . . . I think there's a quotation in one of the books, actually, 'we don't really need any more educated Eichmanns', you know?

The second teacher offers an apparently very different point of view. While expressing concern that 'this might sound a little bit cold', he argues that it is important to treat the Holocaust, 'in a sense like [any] other event' specifically adding, 'I don't want to get in [to] the morality of this'. What just these two extracts also highlight however, is that there is perhaps no simple dichotomy between 'historical' approaches and 'non-historical' – or what these two teachers describe in these instances as 'moral' – aims. A number of teachers in interview described how they encouraged the development of 'historical skills' such as source evaluation and chronology to promote their reflection on precisely 'moral' concerns.

Other teachers appeared to suggest that the Holocaust was something almost outside of history, or 'not just history' both in terms of its gravity and its comparative temporal proximity. For example, in one interview, two history teachers reflected how very differently they would approach teaching about the 'blood and gore' involved in the Battle of Hastings and their teaching of the Holocaust. 'I don't know why I feel like that really,' one concluded,

> I suppose it's because I feel . . . naturally I suppose that the closer in our own time it is the more easy it is to have empathy . . . We don't want them to burst into tears over the fact that Harold got shot in the eye.

History teacher, East Midlands

While the survey asked respondents to choose from a list of suggestions, in interview teachers were simply asked, 'when you teach about the Holocaust, what are your aims?' Their responses indicated a variety of intersecting motivations and intents. Some teachers identified clear and specific teaching aims while others argued that their aims were very difficult to encapsulate or answered in very general or expansive terms. It is instructive to examine the answers teachers gave in interview in relation to those given in response to the survey. Five key areas that emerged from interview discussion are detailed below.

1. Understanding the roots and ramifications of prejudice

It has already been reported that the majority of survey respondents prioritised the aim 'to develop an understanding of the roots and ramifications of prejudice, racism and stereotyping in any society', but a rather more complicated picture emerged from interview. For, although many of the teachers described their aims in relation to precisely the terms 'racism', 'prejudice', and 'stereotyping', very few described an attempt to help students understand the roots of these phenomena. Much more commonly, teaching about the Holocaust was framed as an important opportunity to highlight the ramifications - or 'most extreme' consequence - of racism, prejudice and stereotyping, or more specifically to 'warn against the dangers' of these. In this respect the specific and contingent context of Nazi Germany was scarcely referenced, indeed on occasion it was actively undermined. The Holocaust itself appeared to take the form of an always and everywhere potential danger in many teachers' accounts:

> It's trying to make them realise that it is not something which is one country or one particular set of circumstances - that actually maybe it is something deeper about the human condition. It's something that actually exists within all of us.
>
> History teacher, South East.

The teacher quoted above added that she did not want to locate her students' study too specifically within Nazi Germany in case doing so encouraged anti-German sentiment. Another expressed concern not to 'just package [the Holocaust] away' within a particular place in time.

Another history teacher - who suggested that he always asked his students to consider whether historical analysis could help explain the Holocaust - offered an alternative perspective. Although he began describing his aims by saying that he tried to 'make the point . . . this is where racism can go' he then added, 'this is where it can end up *under certain circumstances*' (emphasis added). It was precisely those 'certain circumstances' – which this teacher described with reference to the actions of individuals and of the German Government – that he considered of most value within a historical approach.

2. Deepening historical knowledge

Only a quarter of history teachers who took part in the survey prioritised the teaching aim, 'to deepen knowledge of World War II and Twentieth Century History'. Yet for many of the history teachers who were interviewed, communicating a factual knowledge of the events of the Holocaust was described as a basic component of what they considered important to accomplish. Indeed, in some interviews it was implied that this aim could be taken for granted, especially as it was often outlined in external exam board specifications or within departmental schemes of work. However, when asked more specifically about their own *personally important* teaching aims, communicating factual knowledge was often not emphasised in the same way.

An exception was one history teacher who reflected:

> I think my aim and objective would be to give them an understanding - a factual understanding - of one of the most important events of the 20th century. Not only because it's important in its own right but because of its impact on the world since. You can't interpret the world without understanding the Holocaust.
>
> History teacher, London

When asked to explain what he meant by the Holocaust's 'impact on the world' his suggestions included 'the creation of the state of Israel, the mindset of the state of Israel'; 'the whole concept of war crimes and how that affects the international world'; and 'the whole way in which Germany was treated after the war'.

More often than not, however, it appeared from the accounts given by teachers in interview that deepening historical knowledge was considered secondary in relation to transmitting bolder and broader aims as described below.

3. 'Transforming society?' Instilling 'moral values', encouraging student action and producing 'good citizens'

The 'transformation of society', promotion of specific values, or inculcation of 'good citizenship' were not explicitly articulated in any of the possible aims to be chosen within the online survey. However, each was regularly emphasised by teachers within interview:

> Our main aim of all that teaching, particularly the Holocaust, is to say we genuinely want to change society.
>
> History teacher, London

> You want to produce children at the end of their schooling . . . who are imbued with moral values and with an ability to be heard.
>
> History teacher, London

> I think it's about tolerance, about understanding diversity, about them respecting one another and each other's views and . . . that actually without that something as drastic as that could happen again.
>
> History and citizenship teacher, West Midlands

In particular, a number of teachers specifically suggested that they wanted to encourage their students to take action against contemporary expressions of prejudice. Again, the notion of an ever-present danger – with the Holocaust as a warning of what can happen when people *do not* respect difference or challenge racism – was regularly invoked.

The popularity within the survey of the aim, 'to learn the lessons of the Holocaust and to ensure that a similar human atrocity never happens again' was also borne out in interview. Yet only one teacher suggested that he asked his students to consider what those lessons were. Other teachers appeared to work with implicit and sometimes difficult to articulate understandings of the 'lessons' they believed their students should learn. In some teachers' accounts the lesson was recognition of the 'fragility of a tolerant society' or that a 'slippery slope' exists 'from bullying to genocide':

> It's kind of, get them to understand that it's not just . . . an isolated experience. And it's certainly not something that just happened in history and will never happen again: that they've actually got to take some active role in that.
>
> Geography teacher, West Midlands

While at least one teacher articulated the potentially rather pessimistic perspective that the key lesson is that humanity cannot learn the lessons of the Holocaust (as evidenced by more recent and ongoing genocides and crimes against humanity), most teachers wanted to encourage students to see themselves as individually important in preventing any comparable atrocity from happening again.

A number of teachers suggested that history itself was a subject which should be experienced 'as a vehicle for transformation' and that a study of the First World War, or the Poor Laws or the Civil Rights Movement in America were also appropriate platforms for inculcating 'good citizenship' or discussing morality. However, these same teachers also expressed a sense that the Holocaust was a particularly apposite arena for this.

4. Emphasising the individual and 'personalising' history

An emphasis on the actions and responsibilities of individuals was another regularly recurring feature of teachers' interviews. 'To explore the roles and responsibilities of individuals, organisations, and governments when confronted by human rights violations and/or policies of genocide', was the third most popular of the aims suggested within the survey (chosen by just over 33%, of teachers who had taught about the Holocaust). However, when describing their teaching aims within interview, the roles of *organisations and governments* were seldom mentioned at all. Instead, the choices and actions of individuals were awarded considerably greater attention, both in terms of the choices and actions of those who lived through the Holocaust and by reflecting on the positions that students themselves would take.

A number of teachers also suggested that one of their key concerns was to 'personalise' and/or 'humanise' the history of the Holocaust. At least two important dimensions of this 'personalisation' were expressed by teachers in interview. From one perspective it was considered important to respect the humanity of the many victims involved by remembering individual stories. But a focus on the individual could also be used to achieve another of the aims suggested by the survey, 'to understand and explain the actions of people involved in and affected by an unprecedented historical event'. This aim was chosen by only 12% of survey respondents with experience of teaching within this area, but more commonly articulated within interview. For example, a number of different teachers suggested that they considered an important aim of their teaching was to emphasise examples of Jewish resistance to the Nazi regime. To do so they considered it was fundamental for students to understand how any individual's choices and actions (or inaction) were influenced by a specific historical context. As one teacher explained, 'I think one of my aims was for pupils to understand why the Holocaust was so difficult to resist'.

In some interviews the concept of empathy was offered in discussions such as these, but again it was used by different teachers in rather different ways. For some teachers, encouraging students' empathy entailed provoking an emotional response when imagining another person's suffering, whereas for others it meant attempting to understand individuals' experience with reference to a wider specific historical context:

> One of the reasons we do that moral dilemmas exercise is so they can actually see, well if you were placed . . . in that position – were you to have to make a choice between saving this person's life or risking your own – what would you necessarily do? And . . . we can see that they usually progress . . . from having the view that it's completely black and white, one side's good and the other side's evil. They actually see that actually it's much more complicated and sophisticated than that.
>
> History and sociology teacher, East Midlands

At one school, a group of history teachers described how they were anxious to avoid 'doing empathy on the Holocaust'. One teacher equated empathy with 'doing imaginative writing' – 'you know, "It was night time and I was scared" which she considered of little value within the history classroom.[25]

5. Moving from 'black and white' understandings and 'opening students' minds'

The notion of helping students move from 'black and white' understandings to 'more complicated and sophisticated' perspectives (as described in the extract above) was employed by teachers in more than one interview. Where these teachers gave further details of precisely what they meant by such 'sophisticated', 'shades of grey', understandings, they often ended up returning to the importance of a detailed, factual knowledge base:

> What I mean is to say, well it wasn't just the Nazis, so you might mention Shakespeare, you might mention the Spanish, you might mention the English during, was it the plague? So you might say there's a historical context there, about antisemitic behaviour . . . You don't necessarily do a great deal of *work* on that, but you do say that that exists, that existed before the 1940s, 1930s.
>
> . . .
>
> The other thing is location, well, the two different sorts of camps . . . So you then give a better understanding of those two: concentration camps perhaps more in Germany and the West, extermination camps in the East. And *why* might that be? . . . The *deeper* understanding is why are they hidden out the way?
>
> History teacher, North East

Another recurring phrase used by teachers was the notion of 'opening minds'. Here the same critical thinking skills that were employed to move away from 'black and white' understandings of the past appeared to be used, by some teachers, to encourage students to reflect on the complex truths behind contemporary concerns. As one teacher suggested, using a study of the Holocaust to 'open students' minds' meant, 'to give them food for thought on current political climates about what's going on'.

Indeed, across all five areas of discussion described above, the relationship between the past and the present – and in particular, the utility of studying the past to make sense of and/or influence the present – was a key concern.

---

[25] Davis, Yeager, and Foster, 2001 op. cit. (n 16).

SUMMARY

This chapter investigated teachers' aims and understandings when approaching the Holocaust. It revealed that the most commonly shared understanding among teachers who took part in the survey is that the Holocaust was the persecution and murder of a range of victims targeted by the Nazi regime. This remained true irrespective of prior teaching experience or subject background. However, the chapter also demonstrated that those teachers who appeared most knowledgeable about the history of the Holocaust were also the most likely to use the term to mean the specific targeting of European Jews. Accounts given by teachers in interview were examined to highlight that, in some cases, teachers purposefully emphasised the non-Jewish victims of Nazi persecution in order to make their teaching more 'relevant' and/or accessible to students in their schools.

The chapter described that many teachers appeared to find it difficult to articulate what – if anything – distinguishes the Holocaust from other genocides. Indeed, in a number of teachers' accounts, the Holocaust was presented in terms of its 'universal' warning. It was also reported that bold, trans-disciplinary aims such as 'understanding the ramifications of racism and prejudice', 'transforming society' and/or 'learning the lessons of the Holocaust to ensure that it never happens again' appeared to be prioritised over distinct and specific disciplinary aims. The next chapter, Chapter 5, further explores the complexities associated with teaching about the Holocaust. In particular it focuses on the opportunities and challenges encountered by teachers when teaching about this difficult and complex subject.

What does the Government want us to be teaching every child of this country? . . . What aspects are they wanting us to teach? What is the focus? . . . What is the outcome they want us to have with the students that we're teaching? . . . Learning from the past or what we can learn in the future? . . . Or is it that they just want us to teach the facts, the figures?

History teacher, London

CHAPTER 5: OPPORTUNITIES AND CHALLENGES WHEN TEACHING ABOUT THE HOLOCAUST

INTRODUCTION

41.3 % (n426) of all teachers who completed the online survey and had experience of teaching about the Holocaust said that they agreed or strongly agreed that it was 'very difficult' to do so effectively (only 36.5%, n358, disagreed or strongly disagreed). This agreement was shared by 43.4% (n246) of history teachers, 36% (n93) of RE teachers, 32.3% (n20) of English teachers, 45.2% (n14) of citizenship teachers and 50% (n12) of teachers of PSHE.

This chapter explores some possible reasons for this reported difficulty. However, when talking with teachers during interview, it became apparent that many were especially enthusiastic and committed to teaching about the Holocaust. Many positive dimensions of teaching practice were also highlighted and discussed. The chapter therefore describes not only 'challenges' but also 'opportunities', both for individual teachers and for the field of Holocaust education as a whole. Discussion is framed around four key areas of interest: time and other curriculum concerns; diversity and prejudice; relationships between staff and students; and training, resources and professional support.

TIME AND OTHER CURRICULUM CONCERNS

Time

The final question asked during interviews with teachers was, 'Do you think there are any specific challenges that could be encountered when teaching about the Holocaust?' Here the single most commonly reported challenge was limited curriculum time. This was echoed by the survey data. Among teachers with experience of teaching about the Holocaust, more agreed with the statement 'I do not have enough curriculum time to teach about the Holocaust effectively' than disagreed (42.8%, n441 compared to 33.5%, n344). These figures were broadly consistent among history teachers (43.5%, n348 agreed and 34.4% disagreed), English teachers (44.1%, n26 compared to 25.4%, n15) and PSHE teachers (33.3%, n8 compared to 16.7%, n4). Concern over curriculum time was most pronounced among citizenship teachers:

58.1% (n18) of these teachers agreed with the statement while 25.8% disagreed. It was least pronounced among RE teachers, equal numbers of whom agreed as disagreed (38%, n98).

In interview, many teachers suggested that this was not necessarily a problem peculiar to teaching about the Holocaust. Indeed, history teachers in particular commonly expressed concern that their whole subject was being 'cut back' in curriculum time. As already reported in Chapter 3, in some schools this resulted in Key Stage 3 history being truncated from a three-year into a two-year course with little or no compulsory history being taught in Year 9. In one school, two history teachers remarked that they now taught only one hour of history each week to all Key Stage 3 year groups and argued that this made it very difficult to build momentum behind any topic or sustain students' interest. At the same time as their classroom hours were being reduced, other history teachers also suggested that they were being asked to deliver more and more, or were being 'pushed' in different directions by what one described as 'initiative overload'. Individuals from other subject areas expressed similar concerns in relation to RE, citizenship and combined humanities.

Although pressure on time was positioned as a general concern affecting *all* history lessons, a number of teachers suggested this had particular consequence for teaching about the Holocaust. Specifically, the Holocaust was characterised by many teachers as a particularly complex subject area. These teachers suggested that considerable care and attention was required to help students work with and process the 'difficult information' that learning about the Holocaust involves. Again, data from the online survey reports that 42.3% (n436) of all teachers with experience in this area agreed that 'devoting insufficient time to teaching about the Holocaust can do more harm than good with respect to what students learn' (only 27.9%, n287, disagreed). As one history teachers described:

> Big, big questions like that are always a challenge to teach, to explore, to explain. Because sometimes you've got to make sure that in a sense you allow sufficient time for conclusions and discussions, [for] people to express themselves. Otherwise, by cutting something perhaps short, it can cause more damage than you've solved.
>
> History Teacher, North East

One of this teacher's colleagues also highlighted 'the difficulty of knowing how much time each individual group is going to need to come to terms with what they are learning about the Holocaust'. He, and many others among those interviewed, emphasised the importance of *flexibility* in the structure of lessons as much as the total availability of classroom time.

Organising content

Among those teachers who saw the Holocaust as a distinctly complex period in history, many suggested that a specific challenge was knowing what content to cover within a limited period of time. These teachers were concerned that their students should reach the end of their work on the Holocaust with an appropriate depth and breadth of understanding but were not always confident in how best to achieve this. Teachers did not want students to leave their classroom thinking that the Holocaust was a story of 'evil Nazis' and 'helpless Jewish victims' but did want to be able to provide some coherence to their units of work. They recognised that in an average of just five or six Key Stage 3 lessons, they could only ever hope to present a partial account.[26]

Some teachers suggested that it was a problem that the National Curriculum did not provide sufficient guidance on this. One teacher in particular said she struggled because she believed she was given too little direction or detail on precisely *what* should be covered and how. She explained that she keenly felt her own responsibility in this area of the curriculum and asked:

> What does the Government want us to be teaching every child of this country? . . . What aspects are they wanting us to teach? What is the focus? . . . What is the outcome they want us to have with the students that we're teaching? . . . Learning from the past or what we can learn in the future? . . . Or is it that they just want us to teach the facts, the figures?

> History teacher, London

Without such guidance, this teacher worried that, within her own department, 'it does feel like the blind leading the blind'.

However, other teachers saw the absence of detailed statutory instruction as an important opportunity and described approaching their lessons on the Holocaust in a different manner to other areas of the history curriculum. Rather than being constrained by thinking, 'oh, I've got to do that for the curriculum – I've got the scheme of work I must do that!' one teacher explained that he tried to encourage himself to 'break the boundaries' when teaching about the Holocaust through, for example, using extended, free-form student discussion and debate.

Teachers' aims and student progress

The perspectives of both of the teachers quoted immediately above relate to another area of potential concern. The first teacher explicitly asked, 'What is the outcome they want us to have?', that is, what is it she should be trying to help her students achieve? One might also ask: how should this teacher judge whether her approach and practice are effective in this area? Are there measurable outcomes that students learning about the Holocaust should achieve?

The perspective of the second teacher, who considered the Holocaust to be an area of enquiry in which it was appropriate to 'break free' of typical curriculum concerns was echoed through a number of interviews. One RE teacher, for example, described that while he had 'set patterns' in how he taught every other unit of his syllabus, 'the minute I teach about the Holocaust it really goes out the window'. Specifically he suggested that he would not necessarily expect his students to produce any written work about the Holocaust and it certainly would not be a unit of work that leant itself to being formally assessed. One of his colleagues from the school's history department agreed:

---

[26] When describing their work with Key Stage 4 and Key Stage 5 students, teachers explained that the specifications produced by examination boards outlined specific content coverage.

> It's taught differently, definitely . . . You can look through [a student's] exercise book and there may not be a great deal there. Because it's not going to be a chalk and talk lesson.
>
> History teacher, North West

In place of formal written work, teachers explained that they wanted to encourage their students to think and reflect, discuss and debate.

Questions of teacher's aims when approaching the Holocaust are again clearly salient here. When asked directly what they wanted their students to achieve through a study of the Holocaust, those teachers who prioritised aims such as 'transforming society' or 'tackling racism and prejudice' were likely to answer in terms which would be very difficult to confidently measure or observe. For example, one teacher reported that she wanted her students to achieve, 'an understanding of how, when it's [left] unchecked, the human race is capable of unspeakable atrocities'. Moreover, she wanted to encourage her students to consider it their 'duty', 'as human beings' to be vigilant against these evils. The same teacher then later reflected:

> I think [attainment targets are] a nonsense when it comes to the Holocaust, I think that's a paper exercise that I regard as completely meaningless here and I think our progress is much more on a personal level with those individual students . . . where you can see them maturing in their thought. And you can't quantify this can you? That's the problem . . . I don't think you can quantify it until they've left school, until they're old enough to reflect back on their experiences.
>
> History teacher, London

In the absence of quantifiable measures of these aspects of students' progress, many teachers suggested that the impact of their teaching would only be observable at some, often unspecified point in the future, if at all. Some teachers did recount the feeling of reward they had experienced on specific occasions when, for example, they saw students drawing their own connections between the Holocaust and contemporary issues, both on a national scale (such as the British reaction to recent asylum seekers and economic migrants) or within their personal lives (such as school-based bullying). Others, however, used a tentative language of what they 'hoped' or were 'trying' to help their students achieve. Observing a similar language used by history and RE teachers in her own (2007) study, Jane Clements describes teachers' 'hope' or 'belief' in the 'deferred benefits' of their work with students in schools. It would be unhelpful to suggest that all valuable learning outcomes must be quantifiable or easy to observe. It is nonetheless a potential challenge if teachers are unclear as to how to judge their students' progress and/or the effectiveness of their own pedagogical approach.

Cross-curricular cooperation and building on work in previous years

Given that many teachers believe their curriculum time is restrictive, it is instructive to consider how teachers might build upon students' learning across different subject areas and/or over successive years. During interview, a number of those history teachers who worked with GCSE and/or A level students emphasised the importance of being able to return to the Holocaust in post-compulsory years in order to examine the subject in greater complexity and depth (of course, only a selection of students – those who choose to study GCSE and/or A level in schools who follow relevant exam board specifications – are given this opportunity). However, few teachers demonstrated in any significant detail how they might build on students' prior learning about the Holocaust in curriculum subjects other than their own. Yet, as already reported from the survey data, students may encounter the Holocaust in a variety of different subject areas, especially in their first years of secondary school.

The teachers who were interviewed were asked if they knew of any other areas in their school's curriculum where teaching about the Holocaust took place. Often teachers answered that they did not know or were unsure. Those who did provide further detail were likely to suggest that they had learned about the activity of colleagues in other departments in an *ad hoc*, almost accidental way. Where teachers from different departments from the same school were interviewed together this appeared to present a valuable and in some cases unprecedented opportunity to learn about each other's pedagogical practice (although it was not always clear in discussion what each subject's specific teaching responsibilities should be).

A small number of history teachers expressed specific concern that colleagues in other departments were introducing students to the Holocaust in Years 7 and/or 8 without any prior discussion or consultation with them. These teachers explained that they believed that an accurate knowledge of the historical events of the Holocaust was vitally important and that the Holocaust was 'safest in the hands of historians'. Arguably, the variations in the scope and accuracy of teachers' historical knowledge about the Holocaust described in Chapter 3, could justify some of these teachers' concerns. In other schools teachers raised the problem of what one characterised as 'Holocaust fatigue'. In one school teachers reported that they had encountered students who, when introduced to a study of the Holocaust, complained, 'oh no, not this again!' These students believed that they had 'done' the Holocaust and had already learned all there was to learn, sometimes on the basis of teaching that had taken place in their primary schools.

It is also important to highlight that in some of the schools visited for interview, potentially very effective and inventive cross-curricular cooperation and division of content was described. In one school, the history and RE departments worked very closely together and had taken the decision to deliver their material on the Holocaust coterminously. This decision was taken in response to complaints from previous years' students who had studied the Holocaust in Year 8 RE and then again in Year 9 history. Now both subjects approached the subject during Year 9 in the run up to Holocaust Memorial Day. On Memorial Day itself they were joined by colleagues from the geography and English departments to run a whole day of activities which culminated with a visit from a survivor of the Holocaust. The teachers suggested that this provided an important opportunity to bring together factual knowledge, historical, theological and philosophical enquiry and ethical as well as political debate.

Discussions with teachers during interviews emphasised that returning to the Holocaust with different year groups – whether in a single subject or across the curriculum – required planning and forethought if students were not to simply perceive (or experience) their teacher's delivery as repetition. In the school described above, one history teacher explained that without such whole school coordination, students,

> think they know it, they think they've done it and then we're doing it again without [them] actually realising the difference of point of view that RS was coming at in Year 8.

History and politics teacher, London

In another school a teacher described his plans to 'plant some of the ideas' that his students would later find helpful in making sense of the Holocaust – for example, the concept of antisemitism and its long history in Europe – at an earlier point in the Key Stage 3 history curriculum. He hoped this would mean he could more effectively make use of the time that he was given when the same students reached Year 9.

DIVERSITY AND PREJUDICE

Cultural diversity

Within the online survey, respondents were asked whether or not they agreed with the statement, 'I find that having students from diverse cultural backgrounds influences the way that I teach about the Holocaust'. Those who agreed were asked to explain in further detail their reasoning. 23.3% (n241) of all respondents with experience of teaching about the Holocaust said they agreed or strongly agreed and 175 respondents contributed further detail. In fact, among these 175 responses, a very wide range of teacher perspectives on classroom diversity was revealed.

A significant proportion of the teachers who responded had taken the opportunity to emphasise that they felt cultural diversity did not – and *should* not – make any difference to the way they taught about the Holocaust, nor any other subject, in school:

> The ethnic mix of a class should have absolutely no bearing on how the Holocaust is taught and nor does it affect my teaching in any way – it doesn't alter the facts in any way.

Extract from survey response

> I do not teach it to draw explicit moral lessons or sermons and so even in a school that is 70% Muslim with strong family links to Palestine, I still take a historical disciplinary perspective and so the cultural background of the class is the same as for all other enquiries.

Extract from survey response

Nevertheless, other teachers used the opportunity to describe a variety of ways in which cultural diversity *did* influence the way they taught about the Holocaust. Some remarked that they purposefully reflected on the presence of minority ethnic students in their classrooms to examine the contemporary salience of the Holocaust or wider 'lessons to be learned'. These teachers suggested that, 'the Holocaust throws up questions of diversity and our reactions to it', 'students need to be taught tolerance and acceptance which is aided by mixing with diverse groups', or:

> [cultural diversity] increases awareness that there are potentially many victims of modern holocausts/genocides or racism and it encourages an awareness of the need to try and empathise.
>
> Extract from survey response

In these teachers' comments, the cultural diversity of students is framed as a resource on which to draw. Some teachers suggested that they directly invited students to share with the rest of the class their own experience of racism and/or prejudice.

Echoing discussion in the previous chapter, a number of the teachers who chose to respond to this question also stated that they believed it was important to make their teaching about the Holocaust 'relevant' to students with different ethnic, national and/or religious backgrounds. For these teachers it was important to draw parallels with other genocides or human rights violations of which pupils in their classrooms may have had first-hand experience. There was also a sense expressed within some of the contributions that teachers believed that some students may feel a closer personal and/or cultural affinity to comparable events other than the Holocaust. In this respect teachers were concerned that students might believe 'their story wasn't being told' and did not want to appear to overlook nor undermine the current and/or historical persecution and prejudice experienced by other groups.

The teacher who remarked that '*even* in a school that is 70% Muslim . . . I take a historical disciplinary perspective' indicates a problematic and growing perception that students from specific national/religious backgrounds are resistant to learning about the Holocaust. In 2007, the Historical Association conducted research with teachers to produce the *Teaching Emotive and Controversial History* or TEACH report (2007b). The words of a small number of teachers at just two of the schools visited by researchers were picked up on when the report was published and were misreported to suggest that the Holocaust was not being taught in English secondary schools because of concerns about the response of Muslim pupils.[27] The data gathered through both the HEDP survey and follow-up interviews *does not* reflect that this is the case. Indeed, a number of teachers in both the survey and interview made an explicit point to reject such an idea. And, while some teachers did report that the culturally framed expectations, beliefs and/or perspectives of students would be a consideration in their teaching, *none* suggested that they had even considered *not* teaching about the Holocaust as a result. A small number of teachers in both the survey and interview suggested that they thought antisemitism and/or Holocaust denial 'might be a potential' issue among certain groups of students, but very few reported having any direct experience of this.

In interview, very few teachers themselves raised the issue of cultural diversity when specifically asked about challenges to teaching about the Holocaust. The individuals

---

[27] The teachers in question were talking about choices they made in terms of topics to include in GCSE (post-compulsory) history but their words were misleadingly interpreted by some to suggest that the position of the Holocaust on the compulsory Key Stage 3 curriculum was under threat.

interviewed were later asked more directly, 'how might the particular group of students that you are teaching influence the approach you take?' At this point, teachers were more likely to talk about variation in students' ability or maturity levels than to raise cultural diversity as an area of concern. Finally, teachers were then asked more directly still, 'what about the cultural background of your students? Could that make a difference to how you teach? In what way?' Here the most commonly given answer was that the presence of German heritage students – and in particular German exchange students – had, on occasion, been difficult for teachers to negotiate.

Dealing with prejudice

Far more commonly than 'cultural diversity', 'cultural homogeneity' was framed as a challenge by teachers in interview. In this respect, students' lack of exposure to cultural difference was seen to lead to problematic (mis)understandings, perspectives and/or prejudice among some ethnic majority students. Again, the importance of having sufficient time to be able to meaningfully explore and potentially challenge students' misunderstandings was emphasised:

> It's very important when we're looking at something like the Holocaust, to actually challenge . . . to have the opportunity to [get them to] think about what they think, [to] think about how they use words.

> If you have two or three students who are quite vocally racist . . . it is important not to let their comments pass unchallenged and that's where it is sometimes quite difficult. Because once you open up . . . something like a discussion on racism, you've got to allow it, not only to take its course, but to ensure that it's finished in a positive way.

> History teacher, North East

As another teacher explained:

> You need to try to understand the mind of a 13 year-old and to understand their value judgements and . . . their emotions and their prejudices before you can tackle them. You do feel like you're opening a mine field – an absolute mine field – which is why it needs the time. You can spend half an hour discussing this . . . particularly if you rise to the challenge and don't pretend you haven't heard.

> History teacher, London

While none of the teachers who were interviewed admitted to 'pretending they hadn't heard', some spoke of 'hoping' that difficult issues did not arise as they were unsure how best to deal with them. Indeed, in some schools, teachers themselves suggested that this was an area in which they could really benefit from clearer guidance and support. Again, the anxieties expressed were not unique to teaching about the Holocaust, but teachers did suggest that they were especially likely to arise in this context.

Another particular challenge identified both explicitly and indirectly by a number of different teachers, was not knowing how best to respond to students' misunderstandings – or lack of understanding – about the nature of 'Jewishness'. Here teachers described feeling particularly ill-equipped to deal with students' questions such as: 'how did [the Nazis] know they were

Jewish?', 'why did Hitler hate them?', or 'why did they admit they're Jewish?' without offering answers that risked reinforcing reductionist stereotypes. One history teacher suggested that this was an area that she believed really benefitted from cross-disciplinary cooperation and that an RE perspective had been very important in helping her develop *her own* – let alone her students' – understanding of how and why the Jews were 'singled out' as a separate and persecuted group.

RELATIONSHIPS BETWEEN TEACHERS AND STUDENTS

Like the history teacher described above, a number of the teachers interviewed positioned *themselves* as uncertain – and regularly 'troubled'- learners in relation to the Holocaust. Some suggested that the Holocaust remained an episode in history that they struggled to understand. Where individuals reflected on their own attempts to make sense of and respond to the Holocaust, this could create interesting relationships of proximity and distance between teachers and the students in their schools. The importance of the quality of relationships between staff and students was indicated by all those teachers who reported that they could not introduce a study of the Holocaust too early in their students' curriculum because they needed to have time to 'really get to know' the class.

Dealing with emotional responses

A small number of those teachers who were interviewed described teaching about the Holocaust in terms of their own continuing 'sadness', 'horror' and even 'dread'. While each of these teachers maintained that they believed the Holocaust was a very important part of their teaching, for them it would always involve emotional discomfort and pain. One suggested that the biggest challenge she faced was 'not crying' in front of students when delivering her lessons and recounted that she had had to 'train' herself in 'taking a step back'. Another teacher, who described the Holocaust as 'horrendously awful' to teach, explained that she refused:

> to watch anything on the television, to read anything, anything at all whatsoever to do with the Holocaust throughout the year . . . I want to come every year fresh to it . . . I don't want to have it in my head too long . . . because I want to take it seriously when I get to it. I don't want to ever become . . . complacent or immunised.
>
> History teacher, North West

This same teacher also revealed that as a consequence she sometimes found her students' reactions very difficult to accept. Each year she declared that she found herself getting increasingly 'cross' because:

> they're so desperately keen to learn about it and it's hard to reconcile as a teacher in your mind, because . . . you're upset because they look like they're enjoying it and you're kind of thinking, well, you shouldn't be enjoying this.
>
> History teacher, North West

A number of teachers interviewed expressed similar anger, frustration or disappointment at what was, from their perspective, students' 'inappropriate' responses. Some worried that their students were becoming 'anaesthetised' to violence – through film and video games, for example – and saw it as a challenge to 'shock' these students into feeling sufficiently 'moved'. Others worried that their teaching could 'traumatise' their students or make them too upset:

> You want to shock, you want to make an impact, but you don't want to upset people too much . . . I mean, they do get upset, and then you'll sit and the bell will go and you say, 'Off you go.' And I don't like sending them out in that kind of a mood. I feel very guilty and I wish I had another hour to kind of say, 'Alright, why are you upset? Let's have a look at it.' And I don't like sending them out to go and do science or maths or art or whatever it is, fresh from that . . . I feel guilty when I start sending them out like that.
>
> RE teacher, North West

This teacher's 'guilt' was one of a variety of complex and sometimes confusing feelings teachers experienced which complicated familiar teacher-student roles. Teaching about the Holocaust appeared to cause teachers to consider their pastoral relationships with students in ways that some had not necessarily experienced before. As one teacher suggested, when teaching about the Holocaust, 'you go into mother mode'.

Confronting the limits of understanding

Student-teacher relationships could also be influenced by the philosophical and/or intellectual challenges of teaching about the Holocaust. For many teachers interviewed a fundamental challenge was the enormity and difficulty of what they were asking students to comprehend:

> There's that famous quote 'the more I study the less I understand'. Because it's such an enormous thing . . . You know, you can't always explain to the kids how or why it happened . . . A lot of time in history it's like 'this all happened and la la la' but I think something of that enormity . . . you know it, but you can't necessarily comprehend it.
>
> History teacher, East Midlands

And unlike in some other areas of history, a number of teachers were not confident that they could provide their students with many concrete answers to complex questions and issues. However, many teachers' also saw this as an opportunity. For example, one history teacher described how he would ask his students,

> 'What do you think my aims should be in this lesson for you?' I've asked them that question, because I think it's a clever way or a good way of getting them to think. To put themselves in my shoes. 'What should I be doing in this lesson?' . . . And I think they actually appreciate it and we feel as if we're together in this.
>
> History and RE teacher, North West

This teacher described how he would position himself alongside his students in his lessons about the Holocaust and suggested that was 'unusual in a history lesson', 'you're usually imparting information and they see you as separate'. Another teacher suggested that the real problems arose when teachers had too clear or rigid an idea of what they wanted their students to take from their learning. From her perspective, the challenge was to give students 'enough space for them to be mature enough and think it through for themselves'. As two teachers remarked, they could give students 'the equipment and critical thinking skills' to address the Holocaust, they could 'immerse' their students in sufficient historical detail, but ultimately they would have to 'stand back and see whether it falls or flies' (Integrated humanities and history teacher, South East).

RESOURCES, PROFESSIONAL SUPPORT AND TEACHER TRAINING

As well as relationships between staff and students, relationships *among* staff, both within and across academic departments, presented both challenges and opportunities. A small number of the teachers who were interviewed described a problematic lack of support from colleagues in other departments who did not understand or recognise the difficult and sensitive nature of teaching about the Holocaust. However, many more teachers emphasised the importance of close collaborative relationships within their teaching teams. In one school, a group of history teachers revealed how their supportive teaching relationships encouraged individuals to come together to reflect on and strategically consider the aims of the department as a whole:

> We're very close in the department so we work very well together [and] that's been ongoing for years and years. So initially someone will be given the responsibility to start the scheme of work and then we'll bring it to the forum and then people will add to it so what I mean is that we're quite happy to not rely on textbooks too much, *we're quite happy to think about our own philosophy and think, where do we want to go with this*? What resources can we make that are going to make it happen?
>
> History teacher, London (emphasis added)

In another school, history teachers suggested that the Holocaust was an area of the curriculum for which it was important to 'liaise' more closely than was normal practice, to learn from each other's experience and to clarify with new members of the department that there were 'certain things we should and shouldn't do' (in this example, teachers were referring in particular to the sensitive use of images, a concern which will be addressed in further detail below). Another teacher noted her difficulty in finding personal time to keep abreast of developments in subject specific and pedagogic literature and emphasised the importance of being able to pool new knowledge and share new understandings that were gained.

Individual's relationships with outside organisations, and in particular teacher training institutions were also significant here. At least two of the teachers interviewed worked closely with local universities to support the professional development of PGCE students and/or NQTs. One history teacher, for example, explained that he often tried to ensure that the PGCE students he mentored were given the opportunity to teach about the Holocaust during their teaching practice within his school. Another teacher described how her work at the university had helped her become more aware of different ways of teaching about the Holocaust. Such connections encouraged teachers to remain reflexive about their teaching practice and to see the Holocaust as an ongoing area of enquiry, rather than something they would ever hope to 'complete'.

A number of teachers who were interviewed also acknowledged the importance of support from a variety of specialist Holocaust education organisations working in the UK. In particular, teachers appeared to value organisational support in arranging visits with students to Holocaust memorial sites and/or museums and in facilitating visits from survivors of the Holocaust to talk to students in schools. Others described how helpful they found some of the resources that such organisations produced. However, data from the online survey would appear to suggest that on a national level, a large number of teachers remain unaware of the various forms of support that are currently available to them and that opportunities for further development exists in this area.

Chapter 3 reported from the online survey data that, in general terms, teachers appear to believe they have sufficient access to effective and appropriate resources to support their teaching about the Holocaust. However, through interview, teachers did raise a number of areas of potential concern. The use of visual images and recorded footage was particularly prominent in discussion here. During one interview, a history teacher with 20 years' experience argued that the growing number of popular films produced about the Holocaust had significantly impacted her own and other people's teaching about the Holocaust. (This is an observation supported by the apparent dominance of *Schindler's List* as the most commonly reported 'useful teaching resource' among teachers who completed the survey). This teacher described that such films had facilitated a move from 'chalk and talk' teaching to a 'more thought-provoking' discussion-based approach.

Elsewhere however, teachers drew attentions to the limitations and/or dangers of using video material in class:

> Sometimes you like to show a video, so you put on something like *Schindler's List*, and . . . it doesn't really have much of an impact because . . . it is too easy to associate it with television and film . . . so, you know, to a 13 or 14 year-old, a film is a film. It's not something that really happened.
>
> History teacher, South East

Other teachers outlined the challenge of knowing how to judge what was appropriate footage to show:

> It is very difficult to find something which is . . . realistic enough to bring it home to them but not so horrifying that you're gonna scare them for life.
>
> History teacher, South East

One teacher was especially concerned that some of the video and photographic footage used in schools had originally been produced by the Nazis to undermine and humiliate their victims. This teacher remarked that, while he wanted his students to be 'shocked and horrified' he was not sure that it was 'morally appropriate' for them to see films which showed, for example, Jewish people being forced to undress before being sent for execution.

The Internet was also identified by teachers as a potentially dangerous resource. Many described using websites and Internet search engines themselves, often to find images and other materials to use in class. However, teachers were wary of their students' reliance on the Internet, especially in the context of the Holocaust. One teacher suggested that his students could be very indiscriminating in the websites they chose to visit and gather information from and was concerned that this exposed them to positions of Holocaust denial.

Finally, a number of teachers described the profound impact – both for themselves and for their students – of hearing survivors of the Holocaust recount their own personal experience. In one school a teacher suggested that, 'having the Holocaust survivors visiting school has given a whole new depth . . . to our understanding as a team'. Her colleague added,

> It just makes it more up to date, you know, it doesn't make it a history thing anymore . . . it makes it actually far more real. And it is within living memory, that's what's so odd about it, you know.

History and sociology teachers, South East

This last teacher's comments raise a further challenge faced by the field of Holocaust education as a whole: what will change when the Holocaust is no longer a period within living memory? During the last ten years, in England as elsewhere in the world, the number of Holocaust survivors willing to visit schools and speak to groups of students has steadily increased. However, the next decade will see a decrease in the number of individuals able to continue sharing their first-hand reflections and memories in this way. Considerable effort by organisations in Britain, Israel and the USA is being expended to record survivors' testimonies and to ensure easy access of the recordings to schools. As Chapter 3 has already reported, both the survey data and school-based interviews suggest that teachers consider eyewitness accounts and personal recollections among the most effective and valuable resources to use with students in schools.

SUMMARY

The primary purpose of this chapter was to explore in more detail the opportunities and challenges teachers encountered when teaching about the Holocaust. It revealed teachers' shared concerns about the lack of curriculum time allocated to its study, the challenges involved in cross-curricular activity and the difficulty of establishing clear aims and learning outcomes. The chapter also provided valuable insights into the importance placed on both nurturing positive teacher-student relationships, to sensitively addressing issues of diversity and prejudice and to providing a supportive and caring environment when teaching about the Holocaust. Of note, echoing the results of the survey, few of the teachers who were interviewed reported having received any specific professional development in teaching about the Holocaust, either during their initial teacher training or at any point subsequently. Again, the majority of teachers reported that they were primarily self-taught. Encouragingly, in respect to the development of CPD programmes in Holocaust education, many teachers suggested that there were specific areas in which they believed it would be very valuable to receive additional professional development and support. Likewise, among the teachers who completed the online survey, 77.5% (n765) said that they would be interested in attending an all-day workshop focused on teaching about the Holocaust. As a consequence, the following brief concluding chapter draws together a number of key findings highlighted within this report and considers their implication for supporting the continuing professional development of teachers in this complex curriculum area.

82.5% of the teachers who took part in the online survey and who had experience of teaching the Holocaust considered themselves self-taught in this area. 77.5% of this same group of teachers indicated that they were interested in attending a workshop for related continuing professional development.

CHAPTER 6: CONSIDERATIONS FOR CPD PROGRAMMES IN HOLOCAUST EDUCATION

INTRODUCTION

This research has reported that currently teachers teach about the Holocaust in a variety of subject areas and across all five compulsory and two post-compulsory year groups in English secondary schools. While the Holocaust is a mandatory component of the National Curriculum for history at Key Stage 3, this report has documented that it also has a significant presence in a number of GCSE and A level options for study in the course specifications currently offered by examinations boards in both England and Wales. Among the 2,108 teachers who took part, the survey captured responses from 591 individuals with experience of teaching about the Holocaust principally in history, 269 with experience of doing so in religious education, 72 in English, 34 in citizenship and 33 in PSHE. This report has described congruence and variation in perspective and practice among and between each of these groups and has combined descriptive analysis of survey data with reflections and accounts offered by 68 teachers in interview.

Although the research deliberately recorded and reports on the views and experiences of teachers from a number of different subject backgrounds, the original intention in commissioning this work was to inform the development of a continuing professional development programme conceived in the first instance to support teachers of history. However, the research has also highlighted the importance of recognising the contribution and commitment of teachers from other subject areas. As reported in Chapter 2, if the survey responses reflect an accurate picture of the landscape of English secondary education, students are likely to be first introduced to the study of the Holocaust in a subject other than history. In addition, given the regularly reported limitations on Key Stage 3 history curriculum time, in Chapter 5 the potential benefits of and challenges to effective cross-curricular cooperation were noted and explored. Reflecting both the original remit of this research and insights gained during its completion, the remainder of this short, concluding chapter reflects on some of its key implications for supporting teachers in this area through a range of CPD activities, including those offered under the auspices of the Holocaust Education Development Programme (HEDP).

VALUING HOLOCAUST EDUCATION

The survey revealed that teachers widely appear to value and support the need to teach about the Holocaust in secondary schools. For example, 85.1% (n889) of those who completed the survey and who had experience of teaching about the Holocaust believe that it is right that the Holocaust is a compulsory part of the secondary school history curriculum. In addition, 94.7% (n1,004) considered that it would always be important to teach about the Holocaust. Despite the existence of these strong sentiments, however, the research suggested that many teachers were uncertain about how to teach about the Holocaust in effective and meaningful ways. In this context it is perhaps revealing that very few teachers who teach about the Holocaust have received any form of specialist training in the subject - with 82.5% (n952) considering themselves self-taught. This lack of formal training in what is a very complex and challenging subject may also explain why 77.5% (n765) of the teachers who took part in the survey indicated they would be interested in attending a workshop for related continuing professional development. In overarching terms, therefore, the research supports the idea that, although many teachers value and appreciate the importance of teaching about the Holocaust, they acknowledge that they would benefit from further professional support.

SUBJECT KNOWLEDGE AND TEACHERS' UNDERSTANDINGS

The Holocaust is the subject of continuing, detailed, academic research and so it is vital that CPD in this area includes opportunities for teachers to update their subject knowledge in ways that can lead to more effective, meaningful and challenging learning experiences for their students. As reported in Chapter 4, this research has shown that there appear to be some areas of teachers' current historical understanding which may be divergent from perspectives shared among a majority of contemporary historians in this field. The Holocaust is clearly a very complex area of historical enquiry but it is also a subject about which many popular conceptions and – more importantly – *mis*conceptions are widely held. Such misconceptions might lead students and their teachers to draw erroneous and misleading conclusions about the actions and behaviours of people in the past. From this perspective, programmes of CPD should seek to equip teachers with the knowledge to challenge shared myths and common-sense assumptions. This would also help teachers avoid over simplistic generalisations that attempt to convey abstract, universal 'lessons'. Arguably, students are likely to have deeper and more valuable understandings about the human condition, about society and about the world around them if their reflections take account of the complexity of the past. Indeed, if students are able to properly contextualise a study of the Holocaust within secure knowledge and understanding of the events of that time they are likely to be better able to relate the Holocaust in meaningful ways to discussions about other genocides and ongoing crimes against humanity.

Furthermore, it may be that updated subject knowledge helps to clarify key issues for teachers regarding definitions, teaching aims and the specific significance of the Holocaust. As described in Chapter 4, a number of teachers found it difficult to articulate what, if anything, gave the Holocaust particular historical and/or educational significance. For these reasons, CPD programmes, including those offered by the HEDP, should encourage teachers to critically consider and explore the following claims:

The Holocaust is an unprecedented historical event

Human history is filled with examples of atrocity and mass murder; there is nothing new about the suffering of the victims of the Holocaust. The Holocaust is unprecedented, however, from the perspective of the ideological and global intent of the perpetrators: this was the first time that a nation state consciously planned to murder every member of a particular group of people (every last man, woman and child), everywhere. It is essential that students and teachers understand how and why this happened in the modern world, and how throughout Europe vast numbers of people perpetrated, collaborated or were complicit in the murder of their Jewish neighbours.

The Holocaust is central to our understanding of modern European society

The Holocaust did not happen long ago, or very far from the United Kingdom. It was a European event in the modern world, at the heart of Western civilization, and stands as a European catastrophe challenging all aspects of our understanding of the development of our society, civilization and cultural development. It is pertinent, therefore, for students and teachers to consider: what went so wrong with how we live together and organise our communities that European society could so quickly and so completely collapse into genocide?

The Holocaust was a paradigmatic genocide

The term 'genocide' did not exist before the Second World War; it was coined as a response to the crimes committed by the Nazis and their collaborators. The Holocaust is therefore central and essential to understandings of the concept of genocide, and to international conventions and legal mechanisms targeted at preventing and punishing crimes that continue to scar our modern world.

The Holocaust occupies a significant position in collective memory

The presence of the Holocaust in our collective memory, in mass media and public discourse, and the use and abuse of Holocaust imagery and motifs in the service of diverse political and social agendas, make it essential for young people's educational literacy and citizenship that they understand this central event of our time, and, under the guidance of well-informed teachers, prove able to critically evaluate these many and diverse cultural representations of the Holocaust.

CURRICULUM TIME

42.8% (n441) of all survey respondents who teach about the Holocaust identify limited curriculum time as an obstacle to effective teaching and learning about the Holocaust. 42.3% (n436) express concern that 'devoting insufficient time to teaching about the Holocaust can do more harm than good with respect to what students learn'. Given the significance and scale of the Holocaust, its complexity and the profound issues that it raises, clearly there is no easy 'fix' to this problem but it is a challenge that any effective CPD in this area must seek to address.

The survey data suggests that certain topics are regularly prioritised for inclusion when teachers approach teaching about the Holocaust, most notably the experiences of individual men, women and children who were persecuted by the Nazis, Auschwitz-Birkenau, propaganda and stereotyping and *Kristallnacht*. Others, such as Operation Reinhard, Jewish social and cultural life before 1933 and the contribution of the Jews to European society and culture appear to be only infrequently included, irrespective of teachers' subject background. Interviews with teachers also indicated that a number lacked confidence and felt uncertain about knowing how to judge precisely which topics to include and exclude in the limited time available to them. This was especially true for Key Stage 3 teachers who, because they were not required to adhere to a GCSE or A level exam specification, were often given relative autonomy over their schemes of work. Through helping teachers develop their specialist knowledge of this period, effective CPD programmes should encourage teachers to consider the historical and educational salience of regularly neglected topics. Moreover, it will support teachers in developing and reflecting upon their own rationale for topic inclusion within the framework of a coherent course of study.

SUBJECT DIVERSITY AND CROSS-CURRICULAR ACTIVITY

Although the research suggests that history is the subject in which the Holocaust is most likely to be taught, the survey data also revealed that teachers from across a range of subjects are keen to explore the Holocaust with young people. The research has also suggested that, in many schools, there may be little whole-school planning on how best to coordinate work across different subject areas. Effective CPD should consider what particular, subject-specific perspectives contribute to young people's learning about the Holocaust and what constitutes an effective cross-curricular or interdisciplinary approach. Moreover, it should provide opportunities and encouragement for teachers to critically examine issues such as these. Clearly moral, theological, historical, philosophical, psychological, geographical, and social questions permeate the study of the Holocaust and meaningful CPD programmes should help teachers to plan, teach and reflect upon their aims and practice with these cross-curricular issues in mind. As well as enriching young people's understandings through multiple disciplinary perspectives, a well co-ordinated approach would also help to avoid duplication and make more effective use of valuable curriculum time.

SUPPORTING EFFECTIVE PEDAGOGY IN CHALLENGING CONTEXTS

During interview, a number of teachers voiced concerns about the dangers of creating or reinforcing negative stereotypes of Jewish people, and of feeding anti-German sentiments that might exist among their students. Effective CPD should support teachers in considering how they challenge prejudiced and stereotyped views, how they manage inappropriate or offensive responses from students and how they can respond most effectively to young people who may deny or trivialise the Holocaust.

Further crucial considerations concern the need to model effective pedagogy, age-appropriate materials, and powerful and engaging classroom strategies and activities. Analysis of the survey and interview data suggests that the Holocaust is a subject likely to cause teachers to confront challenges concerning their sense of responsibility for students' emotional well-being and/or to question their role in the 'moral lessons' their students may or may not learn. An effective CPD programme would help teachers explore how to move young people and how to engage them emotionally, without traumatising them. It would encourage teachers to consider: what activities and resources are effective in engaging students' interest and stimulating enquiry, critical thinking, and deep reflection; how can young people best be supported in the classroom as they encounter stories of mass murder and immense human suffering; what images, historical sources and classroom activities are appropriate to use with students at different age-levels or abilities?

The research indicated that when teachers have had contact with specialist Holocaust education organisations or used their resources, they have found this support very helpful. However the research also suggested that many teachers are not accessing, and may not be fully aware of, the range of resources, expertise and professional guidance on offer to assist teaching in this most complex and challenging area. As a result, effective CPD programmes should help teachers understand what specific forms of support and resources are currently available and, more importantly, provide them with strategies for gauging the ways in which they might benefit from them. This will be a key feature of the HEDP's CPD programme.

WORKING WITH TEACHERS

In addition to support provided by professional, specialist organisations, any CPD programme would be mistaken if it overlooked the significant resource of teachers' own practical experience and classroom expertise. This extensive and detailed national research project has revealed that teachers currently approach teaching about the Holocaust from a number of different perspectives, with different perceptions and understandings and with varying levels of specialist historical knowledge. As Chapter 5 documented, during interviews, many teachers themselves emphasised the value of learning from each other or remarked on the importance of collaborative and supportive teaching teams. As a result of this large-scale study, more is now known about how the Holocaust is taught in English secondary schools than ever before. It is important that this knowledge is not ignored. The HEDP's CPD programme will build upon the understandings and insight provided and will continue to develop through ongoing research and evaluation and, crucially, in response to feedback given by the teachers who take part.

Teachers' own engagement with the process of CPD is of fundamental importance. Indeed, a central feature of the HEDP's programme is the concept of an interactive community of enquiry and exchange. Under the guidance of the HEDP's own specialist educators, teachers will be invited and encouraged to share, discuss and deploy their own developing knowledge and expertise.

In summary, it is hoped that all those engaged in supporting teachers' continuing professional development in Holocaust education will derive benefit from this national study and, more importantly, carefully consider its findings to ensure that teachers are well equipped to teach about the Holocaust to young people in profound, meaningful and effective ways.

APPENDICES

Appendix 1: Final Version of the questionnaire

Question Number	Question/Response text and/or description
1	Sex • Female • Male
2	Age group • 20-25 years • 26-30 years • 31-34 years • 35-40 years • 41-45 years • 46-50 years • 51-55 years • 56-60 years • 61 years and above
3	Ethnicity • White • Mixed • Asian (Indian) • Asian (Pakistani) • Asian (Bangladeshi) • Asian (other) • Black (Caribbean) • Black (African) • Black (other) • Chinese • Prefer not to say
3a	Ethnicity – Other please specify
4a	Religion • Buddhist • Christian (including Church of England, Catholic, Protestant, and all other Christian denominations) • Hindu • Jewish • Muslim • Sikh • No religion • Prefer not to say
4b	Religion – Other please specify
5	In which year did you begin teaching? *drop-down list 2009 – 1940*
6	How many years, in total, have you been teaching? *drop-down list 1-60*
7a	If applicable, which subject have you been (or currently are being) trained in?

	<ul><li>Art & Design</li><li>Citizenship</li><li>Design & Technology</li><li>English</li><li>Geography</li><li>History</li><li>Information & Communication Technology</li><li>Mathematics</li><li>Modern Foreign Languages</li><li>Music</li><li>Physical Education</li><li>PSHE</li><li>Religious Education</li><li>Science</li><li>Work-related Learning</li><li>Not applicable</li></ul>
7b	If applicable, which subject have you been . . . trained in? – Other (please specify)
8a	What do you consider your principal subject? <ul><li>Art & Design</li><li>Citizenship</li><li>Design & Technology</li><li>English</li><li>Geography</li><li>History</li><li>Information & Communication Technology</li><li>Mathematics</li><li>Modern Foreign Languages</li><li>Music</li><li>Physical Education</li><li>PSHE</li><li>Religious Education</li><li>Science</li><li>Work-related Learning</li></ul>
8b	What do you consider your principal subject? – Other please specify
9a	In what type of school do you teach? <ul><li>Academy</li><li>City Technology College</li><li>Community School/College</li><li>Comprehensive</li><li>FE College</li><li>Grammar</li><li>Middle</li><li>School with a religious character (Faith School) [*could you please specify in the box below*]</li><li>Secondary modern</li><li>Sixth form College</li><li>Special</li></ul>
9b	In what type of hcool do you teach? – Other please specify

10	In which Local Authority is your school situated? *drop-down list available with over 150 options*
10a	In which local authority is your school situated? – Other please specify
11	What is your current employment status? • Full-time • Part-time
12a	Many different understandings of the Holocaust exist. From the list tick the box next to the ONE statement that most closely matches your understanding of the Holocaust • The Holocaust was the persecution and murder of a range of victims perpetrated by . . . • The Nazis and their collaborators perpetrated crimes against humanity on millions of people . . . • The Holocaust was the systematic, bureaucratic, state-sponsored persecution and murder of . . . • Hitler believed that ethnic Germans were the members of a 'Master Race'. . . • The persecution of Jewish people during the Second World War . . has been exaggerated . . . • The Holocaust has a universal meaning to describe unspeakable suffering . . • The Holocaust is used in so many different ways, by different groups and individuals . . .
12b	If these options do not closely match your views please add your own in the space below
13a	Listed below are 11 possible aims for teaching about the Holocaust. Please tick the three statements that most closely match the aims you consider to be the most important . . . • to develop an understanding of the roots and ramifications of prejudice, racism, and stereotyping in any society • to reflect upon the theological questions raised by events of the Holocaust • to reflect upon the moral and/or ethical questions raised by events of the Holocaust • to reflect upon political questions, about power and/or abuse of power, raised by events of the Holocaust • to explore the roles and responsibilities of individuals, organisations, and governments when confronted with human rights violations and/or policies of genocide • to deepen knowledge of World War II and Twentieth Century history • to preserve the memory of those who suffered • to understand and explain the actions of people involved in and affected by an unprecedented historical event • to explore questions about the foundations of Western civilisation • to explore the implications of remaining silent and indifferent in the face of the oppression of others • to learn the lessons of the Holocaust and to ensure that a similar human atrocity never happens again
13b	If you would like to comment on these aims, offer your own aims, or explain your rationale further, please use the space below:
14	Please read each of the following questions and indicate a relevant rating

14a	I am confident that I am very knowledgeable about the Holocaust *(strongly disagree/ disagree/ neither agree nor disagree/ agree/ strongly agree)*
14b	I am confident in my preparedness to teach secondary school students about the Holocaust *(strongly disagree/ disagree/ neither agree nor disagree/ agree/ strongly agree)*
15	I have read books on the Holocaust other than school textbooks • Yes • No
16	If yes, and if possible, please list the names of up to three books that you have read that come to mind
16a	Book 1
16b	Book 2
16c	Book 3
17a	Have you personally visited a Holocaust memorial site, research centre or museum within the UK? • Yes • No
17b	If 'yes', please provide further information (e.g. name of site/museum)
18a	Have you personally visited a Holocaust memorial site, research centre or museum outside the UK? • Yes • No
18b	If 'yes', please provide further information (e.g. name of site/museum)
19a	Have you ever participated in a live discussion with (or a presentation by) a Holocaust survivor? • Yes • No
19b	If you remember who this person was, please provide their name
20	Jewish armed revolts occurred in which of the following places: (please tick all that apply) • Amsterdam • Auschwitz-Birkenau • Belzec • Berlin • Paris • Sobibor • Treblinka • Warsaw • not sure
21	Systematic mass murder of Jewish people began in: • 1933, with the Nazis' rise to power • 1935, with the Nuremberg Laws • 1938, with *Kristallnacht* (the November Pogrom) • 1939, with the outbreak of war • 1941, with the Invasion of the Soviet Union • 1942, with the construction of gas chambers at Auschwitz-Birkenau • Not sure

22	Which of the following were killing centres built specifically for killing Jewish people: (please tick all that apply) • Treblinka • Bergen-Belsen • Sobibor • Chelmno • Hadamar • Katyn • Not sure
23	If a member of the German occupying forces refused an instruction to kill Jewish people, the most likely outcome for that individual would be that they were: • Shot for refusing to obey orders • Sent to a concentration camp • Excused from the killing and given other duties • Sent to the Eastern front • Not sure
24	The first group to become victims of a Nazi mass murder programme were: • Disabled people • Jews • Homosexuals • Trade unionists • Jehovah's Witnesses • Black people • Communists • Political opponents of the Nazis • Roma and Sinti ('Gypsies') • Not sure
25	The largest number of Jewish people murdered by the Nazis and their collaborators came from: • Germany • Poland • Ukraine • France • Netherlands • Hungary • Not sure
26	Which of the following statements do you consider best describes the British Government's policy towards Europe's Jews during the Second World War: • Appalled by the atrocities committed by the Nazi regime . . . • The British Government knew that Jewish people and many others in occupied Europe were suffering terribly . . . • The British Government knew about the mass murder programme . . . • Once the British Government knew . . . • The British Government had good knowledge . . . • not sure

27	In percentage terms, the Jewish population in Germany in 1933 was: • fewer than 1% • approximately 5% • approximately 15% • more than 30% • not sure
28	Which of the following statements are accurate with regard to *Kristallnacht*. (please tick all that apply) • *Kristallnacht* occurred on 9-10 November 1938 • The attack was spontaneous and unauthorised • The destruction occurred mainly in large cities and towns • The perpetrators were Nazi thugs who were fined for the damage caused during the attacks • The cooperation of ordinary people in the atrocities occurred primarily in Vienna • The events of *Kristallnacht* led to a brief but intense burst of opposition to the Nazis from the German people • The only world leader to publicly condemn the events of *Kristallnacht* was Franklin D. Roosevelt • The events of *Kristallnacht* were used to justify the introduction of a series of antisemitic laws to which few citizens objected • Over 90 Jews were killed and approximately 200 synagogues destroyed • not sure
29	Please respond to the following statements • My Initial Teacher Training course included a specific focus on teaching about the Holocaust *(No/Not sure/Yes)* • I received formal training in teaching about the Holocaust during my NQT year/first year of teaching *(No/Not sure/Yes)* • I have taken part in training (departmental, INSET, CPD) to support my teaching about the Holocaust, since becoming a teacher *(No/Not sure/Yes)* • I have taken part in training courses in Holocaust education offered by organisations from outside my school *(No/ Not sure/Yes)* • Since becoming a teacher I have taught myself how to approach teaching the Holocaust *(No/Not sure/Yes)* • Since becoming a teacher I have had informal training in teaching about the Holocaust *(No/Not sure/Yes)*
30	A number of organisations involved in Holocaust Education provide support and training for teachers. If possible, please list up to three that come to mind
30a	Organisation 1
30b	Organisation 2
30c	Organisation 3
31	If applicable, please provide the name of the most recent training course in Holocaust Education in which you have participated
32	If applicable, please provide the year of the course *drop-down list available, 2009-1945*

33	If applicable, please provide the duration of the course
	<ul><li>0.5 day</li><li>1 day</li><li>2 days</li><li>3 days</li><li>4 days</li><li>5 days</li><li>6 days</li><li>7 days or more</li></ul>
34	If applicable, please rate the impact of the course on your practice The course had a clear impact on my practice: *(strongly disagree/disagree/neither agree nor disagree/agree/strongly agree/N.A.)*
35	Which of the following statements best describes your practice?<ul><li>I have never taught about the Holocaust</li><li>I have taught about the Holocaust during the past three years</li><li>Although I haven't taught about the Holocaust during the last three years, I have taught about it in the past</li></ul>
36	There are many reasons why you may not have taught about the Holocaust. From the list below please tick all that apply<ul><li>In my school it is considered to be too controversial a topic</li><li>In my school it is not considered to be a key part of the courses that I teach</li><li>In my school there are too many other curriculum pressures and demands and there is not enough time to include this topic</li><li>In my school it is considered to be too emotionally difficult a topic</li><li>We do not have the necessary teaching materials in my school</li><li>My school considers it to be too intellectually demanding a topic</li><li>It is not part of our schemes of work</li><li>I am not personally interested in the topic</li><li>I find the topic too emotionally upsetting</li><li>I am not confident that I have the necessary subject knowledge</li><li>I am not confident in my ability to teach sensitive and emotive issues of this nature</li><li>I feel that this topic is very well publicised already (for example in the media) and there is no need for me to focus on it</li><li>I am concerned that teaching about this topic may increase antisemitism</li><li>I am concerned that teaching about this topic may cause anti-German feeling</li><li>I feel that there are many more positive topics in Jewish history to teach about and I prefer to focus on these</li><li>I feel that this topic is very much in the past and that it has little contemporary relevance</li><li>I do not teach any year groups in which the Holocaust is taught</li><li>I am worried that students will find the subject too emotionally upsetting</li><li>I am worried that my students will find this topic too controversial</li><li>I am worried that students will react inappropriately, or fail to take this seriously</li></ul>
36a	Other (please specify)

37	In which subject do you principally teach about the Holocaust
	• English
	• Mathematics
	• Science
	• Art & Design
	• Citizenship
	• Design & Technology
	• Geography
	• History
	• Information & Communication Technology
	• Modern Foreign Languages
	• Music
	• Physical Education
	• Work-related Learning
	• Religious Education
	• PSHE
37a	Other (please specify)
38	If applicable, please list any other school subject(s) in which you teach about the Holocaust (tick all that apply)
	• English
	• Mathematics
	• Science
	• Art & Design
	• Citizenship
	• Design & Technology
	• Geography
	• History
	• Information & Communication Technology
	• Modern Foreign Languages
	• Music
	• Physical Education
	• Work-related Learning
	• Religious Education
	• PSHE
38a	Other (please specify)

39	Focusing on your principal subject, how much time do you spend on teaching about the Holocaust in hours for each year group? Also, please indicate in which term you are most likely to teach about the Holocaust. • Year 7 - Hours per school year (*drop-down list 1-75*) • Year 7 – Term (*Autumn, Spring, Summer*) • Year 8 - Hours per school year (*1-75*) • Year 8 – Term (*Autumn, Spring, Summer*) • Year 9 - Hours per school year (*1-75*) • Year 9 – Term (*Autumn, Spring, Summer*) • Year 10 - Hours per school year (*1-75*) • Year 10 – Term (*Autumn, Spring, Summer*) • Year 11 - Hours per school year (*1-75*) • Year 11 – Term (*Autumn, Spring, Summer*) • Year 12 - Hours per school year (*1-75*) • Year 12 – Term (*Autumn, Spring, Summer*) • Year 13 - Hours per school year (*1-75*) • Year 13 – Term (*Autumn, Spring, Summer*)
40	When planning to teach about the Holocaust with which other subject areas have you co-operated? (please tick all that apply) • Art & Design • Citizenship • Design & Technology • English • Geography • History • Information & Communication Technology • Mathematics • Modern Foreign Languages • Music • Physical Education • PSHE • Religious Education • Science • Work-related Learning • None
40a	Other (please specify)

41	Please read each of the following statements and indicate the extent to which you agree with them
	• I try to give students key facts and information about the Holocaust, providing them with a clear narrative outline (strongly disagree/disagree/neither agree nor disagree/agree/strongly agree)
	• When teaching about the Holocaust I emphasise the horror of those events and the human suffering – I want students to have a deep emotional response to this topic (strongly disagree/disagree/neither agree nor disagree/agree/strongly agree)
	• I use testimony and individual stories to encourage students to engage with this subject on an empathetic level (strongly disagree/disagree/neither agree nor disagree/agree/strongly agree)
	• When teaching about the Holocaust I take a disciplinary approach and focus on historical teaching (strongly disagree/disagree/neither agree nor disagree/agree/strongly agree)
	• When teaching about the Holocaust I allow time for debate and discussion (strongly disagree/disagree/neither agree nor disagree/agree/strongly agree)
	• When teaching about the Holocaust I adopt a source-based 'skills' approach (strongly disagree/disagree/neither agree nor disagree/agree/strongly agree)
	• When teaching about the Holocaust I take an enquiry-based approach and work to address big questions (strongly disagree/disagree/neither agree nor disagree/agree/strongly agree)
	• When teaching about the Holocaust I ask students to consider theological questions (strongly disagree/disagree/neither agree nor disagree/agree/strongly agree)
	• When teaching about the Holocaust I ask students to consider moral and/or ethical questions (strongly disagree/disagree/neither agree nor disagree/agree/strongly agree)
	• When teaching about the Holocaust I engage students in political questions about power and/or the abuse of power (strongly disagree/disagree/neither agree nor disagree/agree/strongly agree)
	• When teaching about the Holocaust I start with students' perceptions and understandings of the Jewish community today (strongly disagree/disagree/neither agree nor disagree/agree/strongly agree)
	• Holocaust denial has no legitimacy and should have no place in the classroom, hence I do not teach about it (strongly disagree/disagree/neither agree nor disagree/agree/strongly agree)
	• I consider all perspectives about the Holocaust in a balanced way, including Holocaust denial (strongly disagree/disagree/neither agree nor disagree/agree/strongly agree)
	• I teach about Holocaust denial to expose it as antisemitic propaganda (strongly disagree/disagree/neither agree nor disagree/agree/strongly agree)
	• I teach about the Holocaust to encourage student action on current human rights issues (strongly disagree/disagree/neither agree nor disagree/agree/strongly agree)
	• I do not have enough curriculum time to teach about the Holocaust effectively (strongly disagree/disagree/neither agree nor disagree/agree/strongly agree)
	• I think it will always be important to teach about the Holocaust (strongly disagree/disagree/neither agree nor disagree/agree/strongly agree)
	• I think the Holocaust will become less relevant to our daily lives as the events

<table>
<tr><td></td><td>

of that time recede further into the past (strongly disagree/disagree/neither agree nor disagree/agree/strongly agree)

- I think that it is right that teaching about the Holocaust is compulsory in the history school curriculum (strongly disagree/disagree/neither agree nor disagree/agree/strongly agree)
- I think that teaching about the Holocaust should be compulsory in one or more other subject areas (strongly disagree/disagree/neither agree nor disagree/agree/strongly agree)
- I think the Holocaust gets too little attention, relative to other topics (strongly disagree/disagree/neither agree nor disagree/agree/strongly agree)
- I think that it is very difficult to teach about the Holocaust effectively (strongly disagree/disagree/neither agree nor disagree/agree/strongly agree)
- The Holocaust is clearly very important but so are other genocides and crimes against humanity: these should get similar curricular time and attention (strongly disagree/disagree/neither agree nor disagree/agree/strongly agree)
- I think the Holocaust is more important than most other topics I teach (strongly disagree/disagree/neither agree nor disagree/agree/strongly agree)
- I think that devoting insufficient time to teaching about the Holocaust can do more harm than good with respect to what students learn from it (strongly disagree/disagree/neither agree nor disagree/agree/strongly agree)
- I find that having students from diverse cultural backgrounds influences the way that I teach about the Holocaust (strongly disagree/disagree/neither agree nor disagree/agree/strongly agree)

</td></tr>
<tr><td>41a</td><td>If you agree/strongly agree with the last statement, please explain why</td></tr>
<tr><td>42</td><td>

Due to time and other constraints, teachers are often restricted in what they are able to cover. When teaching about the Holocaust, which of the following do you include in your teaching?

- The long history of antisemitism (*never/.../.../.../always*)
- Jewish social and cultural life before 1933 (*never/.../.../.../always*)
- The contribution of the Jews to European social and cultural life before 1933 (*never/.../.../.../ always*)
- National Socialist Ideology (*never/.../.../.../always*)
- The Nuremberg Laws (*never/.../.../.../always*)
- Neo-Nazism (*never/.../.../.../always*)
- *Kristallnacht* (*never/.../.../.../always*)
- The experiences of individual men, women and children who were persecuted by the Nazis (*never/.../.../.../always*)
- The impact of the policies of the Christian Churches (*never/.../.../.../always*)
- The choices and actions of bystanders (*never/.../.../.../always*)
- The choices and actions of rescuers (*never/.../.../.../always*)
- The reaction of countries around the world to Jewish refugees (*never/.../.../.../always*)
- The Katyn Massacre (*never/.../.../.../always*)
- An account of life in the Polish ghettos (e.g. Lodz) (*never/.../.../.../always*)
- Resistance to Nazi policies by Jewish partisans (*never/.../.../.../always*)
- Operation Reinhard (*never/.../.../.../always*)
- The *Einsatzgruppen* (*never/.../.../.../always*)
- The Wannsee Conference (*never/.../.../.../always*)
- Auschwitz-Birkenau (*never/.../.../.../always*)

</td></tr>
</table>

	• Jewish resistance in the camp system (*never/.../.../.../always*)
	• The Warsaw Ghetto Uprising (*never/.../.../.../always*)
	• Post-war justice and the Nuremberg trials (*never/.../.../.../always*)
	• The experiences of Holocaust survivors since 1945 (*never/.../.../.../always*)
	• Changes in awareness and understanding of the Holocaust since 1945 (*never/.../.../.../always*)
	• The impact of the Holocaust on the Declaration of Human Rights (*never/.../.../.../always*)
	• Propaganda and stereotyping (*never/.../.../.../always*)
	• Combating current racist ideology (*never/.../.../.../always*)
	• The study of World War II (*never/.../.../.../always*)
	• The study of Hitler's rise to power and the Nazi State (*never/.../.../.../always*)
	• The Arab/Israeli conflict (*never/.../.../.../always*)
	• Other genocides (*never/.../.../.../always*)
	• Exploring the concept of suffering (*never/.../.../.../always*)
	• Human motivation and behaviour (*never/.../.../.../always*)
	• The Holocaust as an unprecedented event in human history (*never/.../.../.../always*)
	• Holocaust related events (e.g. Holocaust Memorial Day) (*never/.../.../.../always*)
43	<u>Are there any resources that you find particularly useful/effective in teaching about the Holocaust? Could you please name three in order of value/effectiveness</u>
43a	Resource 1
43b	Resource 2
43c	Resource 3
44	<u>'Taking into account the opportunities and restrictions at my school, when teaching about the Holocaust I...'</u> • invite a Holocaust survivor to talk to my students (*never/.../.../.../always*) • invite experts and/or guest speakers to talk about the Holocaust (*never/.../.../.../always*) • incorporate visits to a memorial site, research centre or museum within the UK (*never/.../.../.../always*) • incorporate visits to a memorial site, research centre or museum outside of the UK (*never/.../.../.../always*) • use feature films about the Holocaust (*never/.../.../.../always*) • use TV/Film documentaries about the Holocaust (*never/.../.../.../always*) • use docudrama about the Holocaust (*never/.../.../.../always*) • use the Internet to research the Holocaust (*never/.../.../.../always*) • use the Internet in the classroom (*never/.../.../.../always*) • use school textbooks (*never/.../.../.../always*) • use the QCA scheme of work (*never/.../.../.../always*) • use museum resource packs (*never/.../.../.../always*) • use resource packs from Holocaust Education organisations (*never/.../.../.../always*) • use in-school produced study packs (*never/.../.../.../always*) • use what I can find in the department (*never/.../.../.../always*) • have adequate educational resources (*never/.../.../.../always*) • use resources that I developed from my own reading (other than textbooks) (*never/.../.../.../always*)

45	Would you find it useful to have additional support or training to help you teach about the Holocaust more effectively? *(Yes/ Possibly/No)*
45a	If you selected 'No', please explain why in the box below
46	If you answered 'yes' or 'possibly' to the previous question, what types of support or training would you find useful? Please tick all that apply: • Exemplary lesson plans and/or schemes of work • High quality visual resources for the classroom (e.g. DVDs, films, photographs) • High quality written resources (booklets, activities, documentary sources) • High quality Internet-based activities and enquiries for students • High quality online support and resources for teachers • Attendance at high quality all-day workshop(s), led by a specialist in Holocaust Education • The opportunity to participate in high quality accredited continuing professional development (CPD) in Holocaust Education
46a	Other (please specify)
47	If a 'workshop' was offered in a regional centre near you, would you be interested in attending? • Yes, definitely • Yes, probably • Possibly • No, probably not • No, definitely not
48	If you answered 'yes' or 'possibly', to what extent would you find it likely to receive 'cover' from your school in order to participate in such a workshop? • Impossible • Quite unlikely • Not sure • Probably • Definitely
49	If you answered 'no', please explain in the box below why you would not want to participate in the workshops
50	If you have any other general comments, please use the comment box below
51	Would you be willing to participate in a follow-up interview?
52	Name
53	Telephone number
54	Email Address

Appendix 2: Consultation with professional educators, stakeholders and national and international experts in Holocaust education.

In the development and design of the research representatives from Holocaust education agencies and other related organisations provided support and advice to the HEDP team during two stakeholder meetings hosted at the IOE. The following organisations contributed to this process of consultation.

- Anne Frank Trust UK
- Department for Children, Schools and Families
- Facing History and Ourselves
- Historical Association
- Holocaust Educational Trust
- Holocaust Memorial Day Trust
- Imperial War Museum
- Jewish Museum London
- London Jewish Cultural Centre
- Office for Standards in Education
- The Holocaust Centre
- The Pears Foundation
- Training and Development Agency for Schools
- Qualifications and Curriculum Authority
- University of Hull
- University of Nottingham
- University of Southampton
- University of Strathclyde
- University of West Scotland
- University of Wolverhampton
- Wiener Library

The research also benefited from the guidance and advice of academics and historians including:

Stephen Feinberg, United States Holocaust Memorial Museum
Dr Wolf Kaiser, The House of the Wannsee Conference
Christer Mattsson, The Living History Forum
Dorit Novak, The International School for Holocaust Studies, Yad Vashem
Dr Geoffrey Short, University of Hertfordshire
Dr Stephen Smith & Dr James Smith, The Holocaust Centre
Professor Dan Stone, Royal Holloway, University of London

And other professionals in the field including:

Thamar Barnett
Helen Hyde
Dr Karen Murphy
Vanessa Ogden

Furthermore, academic staff with expertise in history, citizenship, and religious education, all based at the Institute of Education, provided invaluable support:

Arthur Chapman (history)
Christopher Edwards (history)
Jeremy Hayward (citizenship)
Professor Chris Husbands (history)
Alison Kitson (history)
Jo Pearce (RE)

Finally, the HEDP received guidance, support and advice from a number of Holocaust survivors. Their contribution is particularly valued:

Ben Helfgott, MBE
Anita Lasker-Wallfisch
Zigi Shipper
Mala Tribich

Appendix 3: Consultation with Holocaust Education Agencies and Related Organisations

- Anne Frank Trust UK

- Facing History and Ourselves

- Historical Association

- Holocaust Educational Trust

- Imperial War Museum

- Jewish Museum London

- London Jewish Cultural Centre

- The Holocaust Centre

- The Pears Foundation

- Teacher Development Agency for Schools

Appendix 4: Members of the HEDP Advisory Board

The HEDP Advisory Board consists of representatives of the Department for Children, Schools and Families (DCSF), the Institute of Education (IOE), The Pears Foundation, and the Holocaust Educational Trust (HET).

In addition to academic and professional staff from the IOE, at the time the research was conducted, the principal members of the HEDP Advisory Board were:

- Lisa Capelouto, The Pears Foundation
- Amy Philip, The Pears Foundation
- Karen Pollock, HET
- Elaine Schollar, DCSF
- Barbara Tucker, DCSF

Appendix 5: Possible Topics that could be Included in a Study of the Holocaust

As part of the online survey, those teachers who had already reported that they were currently teaching or had previously taught about the Holocaust were presented with a list of 35 possible topics that could be included in a study of the Holocaust. Teachers were asked to indicate which they themselves included, marking each along a five-point scale from those they 'never' included to those that they would 'always' include. The table below ranks all 35 topics on the basis of how many teachers reported that they were more likely than not to be included within their teaching.

Ranking	No. of Teachers	Topic
1	900	The experiences of individual men, women and children who were persecuted by the Nazis
2	875	Auschwitz-Birkenau
3	801	Propaganda and stereotyping
4	701	*Kristallnacht*
5	671	The choices and actions of bystanders
6	606	The Nuremberg Laws
7	604	The choices and actions of rescuers
8	600	The study of Hitler's rise to power and the Nazi State
9	595	Combating current racist ideology
10	573	An account of life in the Polish ghettos (e.g. Lodz)
11	567	Human motivation and behaviour
12	549	Holocaust-related events (e.g. Holocaust Memorial Day)
13	548	National Socialist Ideology
14	545	The study of World War II
15	524	The long history of antisemitism
16	509	Other genocides
17	497	The Holocaust as an unprecedented event in human history
18	484	The Warsaw Ghetto Uprising
19	476	Exploring the concept of suffering
20	455	Jewish resistance in the camp system
21	454	The Wannsee Conference
22	425	The *Einsatzgruppen*
23	414	The reaction of countries around the world to Jewish refugees
24	409	The experiences of Holocaust survivors since 1945
25	374	Post-war justice and the Nuremberg trials
26	363	Resistance to Nazi policies by Jewish partisans
27	323	The impact of the policies of the Christian Churches
28	294	Neo-Nazism

29	267	Changes in awareness and understanding of the Holocaust since 1945
30	262	The impact of the Holocaust on the Declaration of Human Rights
31	260	Jewish social and cultural life before 1933
32	256	The contribution of the Jews to European social and cultural life before 1933
33	200	The Arab/Israeli conflict
34	119	Operation Reinhard
35	50	The Katyn Massacre

References

Bankier, D., 1992. *The Germans and the Final Solution. Public opinion under Nazism.* Oxford: Blackwell.

Bartov, O., 2000. *The Holocaust: Origins, implementation, aftermath.* London: Routledge.

Bauer, Y., 2001. *Rethinking the Holocaust.* Yale Nota Bene: New Haven.

BERA, 2004. *Revised ethical guidelines for educational research.* Southwell: British Educational Research Association.

Brown, M. & Davies, I., 1998. 'The Holocaust and education for citizenship: the teaching of history, religion and human rights in England', *Educational Review,* 50 (1), pp. 75-83.

Browning, C. R., 1992. *Ordinary men: Reserve Police Battalion 101 and the Final Solution in Poland.* New York: HarperCollins.

Browning, C.R., 2004. *The Origins of the Final Solution: The evolution of Nazi Jewish policy September 1939-March 1942.* Jerusalem: Yad Vashem.

Burtonwood, N., 2002. 'Holocaust Memorial Day in schools – context, process and content: a review of research into Holocaust education', *Educational Research,* 44 (1), pp. 69-82.

Carrington, B. & Short, G., 1997. 'Holocaust Education, anti-racism and citizenship', *Educational Review,* 49 (3), pp. 271-82.

Cesarani, D., 2004. *Eichmann: His life and crimes.* London: Heinemann.

Clements, J., 2006. 'A very neutral voice: teaching about the Holocaust', *Educate,* 5 (2) [*online*]. Available at: http://www.educatejournal.org/index.php?journal=educate&page=article&op=view&path%5B%5D=60&path%5B%5D=56 [Accessed 30 March 2009].

Clements, J., 2007. *Difficult knowledge: Possibilities of learning in Holocaust education.* Ph.D. London: Institute of Education, University of London.

Crawford, K. A., 1996. 'A history of the right: the battle for National Curriculum history 1989-1994'. *British Journal of Educational Studies,* 43, pp. 12-24.

CRE, 2002. Towards *racial equality: An evaluation of the public duty to promote race equality and good race relations in England and Wales* [online]. Available at: http://www.equalityhumanrights.com/uploaded_files/PSD/research_doc_towards_racial_equality.pdf [Accessed 20 July 2009].

CST, 2008. *Antisemitic incidents report* [online]. Available at: www.thecst.org.uk [Accessed 20 July 2009].

CST, 2009. *Antisemitic incidents* [online]. Available at: www.thecst.org.uk [Accessed 20 July 2009].

Davis, O. L., Jr., Yeager, E. A., and Foster S. J. (eds), 2001. *Historical empathy and perspective taking in the social studies.* Lanham, MD: Rowman and Littlefield Publishers, Inc.

DCSF, 2008a. *School workforce in England. [pdf]* London: DCSF. Available at: http://www.dcsf.gov.uk/rsgateway/DB/SFR/s000787/SFR10_2008.pdf [Accessed 30 March 2009]

DCSF, 2008b. '*DCSF: GCSE and equivalent results in England, 2007/08 (Provisional)'.* Available at: http://www.dcsf.gov.uk/rsgateway/DB/SFR/s000826/index.shtml [Accessed 14 June 2009].

DCSF, 2008c. '*DCSF: GCE/VCE A/AS and equivalent examination results in England, 2007/08 (Provisional)'.* Available at http://www.dcsf.gov.uk/rsgateway/DB/SFR/s000816/index.shtml [Accessed 14 June 2009].

Dickinson, A., 2000. 'What should history be?'. In A. Kent (ed). *School subject teaching: The history and future of the curriculum.* London: KoganPage.

Foster, S. J., 1998. 'Politics, parallels, and perennial curriculum questions: The battle over school history in England and the United States'. *The Curriculum Journal,* 9, pp. 153-164.

Fox, J. P., 1989. *Teaching the Holocaust: the report of a survey in the United Kingdom (1987).* The National Yad Vashem Charitable Trust and the Centre for Holocaust Studies, University of Leicester.

Foxman, A.H., 2008. *Financial crisis brings out the anti-semites.* Available at: http://www.adl.org/ADL_Opinions/Anti_Semitism_Global/JPost_101308.htm [Accessed 2 July 2009].

Friedlander, H., 1998. 'The T4 Killers. Berlin, Lublin, San Sabba'. In M. Berenbaum, (ed). *The Holocaust and history. The known, the unknown, the disputed and the re-examined.* Indiana: University Press.

Friedländer, S., 2007. *The years of extermination: Nazi Germany and the Jews 1939 -1945.* New York: Harper Collins.

Goldhagen, D., 1996. *Hitler's willing executioners: Ordinary Germans and the Holocaust.* New York: Alfred A. Knopf.

Hansard, 2009. "Teachers: Gender" (HC Deb), 20 April 2009, c282W. Available at: http://www.theyworkforyou.com/wrans/?id=2009-04-20g.267743.h [Accessed 2 July 2009].

Harris, R. & Foreman-Peck, L., 2004. 'Stepping into other peoples' shoes': Teaching and assessing empathy in the secondary history curriculum. *International Journal of Historical Learning, Teaching and Research. Available at:* http://centres.exeter.ac.uk/historyresource/journal8/8contents.htm [Accessed 21 July 2009].

Haydn, T., 2004. 'History'. In J. White (ed). *Rethinking the school curriculum.* London: Routledge Falmer.

Hector, S., 2000. 'Teaching the Holocaust in England'. In: I. Davies, ed. *Teaching the Holocaust.* London: Continuum.

Howson, J., 2009. Potential and pitfalls in teaching 'big pictures' of the past. *Teaching History,* 136, pp. 24-33.

ITF, 2004. *Handbook for teachers. Guidelines for teaching about the Holocaust. Documents of the Education Working Group* [online]. Available at: http://taskforce.ushmm.org [Accessed 21 July 2009].

ITF, 2006. *United Kingdom - Holocaust education report* [online]. Available at: http://www.holocausttaskforce.org/education/holocaust-education-reports/53.html [Accessed 27 March 2009].

Kinloch, N., 1998. Learning about the Holocaust: Moral or historical question? *Teaching History, 93, pp. 44-46.*

Kushner, T., 1994. *The Holocaust and the liberal imagination. A social and cultural history.* Oxford: Blackwell.

Landau, R., 1992. *The Nazi Holocaust, its history and meaning.* London: IB Tauris & CoLtd.

Lange, A., 2008. *A survey of teachers' experiences and perceptions in relation to teaching about the Holocaust.* The Living History Forum. Stockholm: Elanders Golab.

Lee, P., 1984. 'Why learn history?'. In A. Dickinson et al (eds). *Learning history.* London: Heinemann.

Lee, P., 1991. 'Historical knowledge and the National Curriculum'. In R. Aldrich (ed). *History in the National Curriculum.* London: Kogan Page in association with the Institute of Education, University of London.

Lee, P., Shemilt, D., Slater, J., Walsh, P., & White, J., 1992. *The aims of school history: The National Curriculum and beyond.* London: the Tufnell Press in association with the Institute of Education, University of London.

Lee, P. & Howson, J., 2006. 'Two out of five did not know that Henry VIII had six wives'. In L. Symcox and A. Wilschut (eds). *National history standards: The problem of the canon and the future of teaching history.* Greenwich, CT.: Information Age Publishing.

London, L., 2003. *Whitehall and the Jews, 1933-1948: British immigration policy, Jewish refugees and the Holocaust.* Cambridge: Cambridge University Press.

Maitles, H. & Cowan, P., 2007. 'Does addressing prejudice and discrimination through Holocaust education produce better citizens?', *Educational Review*, 59 (2), pp. 115-130.

PCAA, 2007. *Report of the all party parliamentary inquiry into antisemitism: Government response* [online]. Available at: http://www.thepcaa.org [Accessed 21 July 2009].

PCAA, 2008. *Government response one year on progress report* [online]. Available at: http://www.thepcaa.org [Accessed 21 July 2009].

Phillips, R., 1998. History teaching, nationhood, and the state: A study in educational politics. London: Cassell.

QCA, 2007. *History programme of study for key stage 3 and attainment target.* Available at: http://curriculum.qca.org.uk/key-stage-3and-4/subjects/history/index.aspx [Accessed 21 July 2009].

Russell, L., 2006. *Teaching the Holocaust in school history.* London: Continuum.

Salmons, P., 2001. Moral dilemmas: history teaching and the Holocaust. *Teaching History,* 104, pp. 34-40.

Salmons, P., 2003. 'Teaching or preaching? The Holocaust and intercultural education in the UK', *Intercultural Education,* 14 (2), pp. 139-149.

Shemilt, D., 2009. 'Drinking an ocean and pissing a cupful: how adolescents make sense of history'. In L. Symcox and A. Wilschut (eds). *National history standards: The problem of the canon and the future of teaching history.* Greenwich, CT. Information Age Publishing.

Short, G., 1991. Combating antisemitism. Dilemma for antiracist education. *British Journal of Educational Studies,* 39 (1), pp. 33-44.

Short, G., 1994a. 'Teaching about the Holocaust: a consideration of some ethical and pedagogic issues', *Educational Studies,* 20 (1), pp. 53-67.

Short, G., 1997. 'The role of the Holocaust in antiracist education: a view from the United Kingdom', *New Community,* 23 (1), pp. 75-88.

Short, G., 2005. 'Learning from genocide? A study in the failure of Holocaust education?'. *Intercultural Education,* 16 (4), pp. 367-380.

Short, G. & Reed, C. A., 2004. *Issues in Holocaust education.* Ashgate: Aldershot.

Slater, J., 1989. The politics of history teaching: A humanity dehumanized? London: Institute of Education.

Supple, C., 1992. *The teaching of the Nazi Holocaust in North Tyneside, Newcastle and Northumberland secondary schools.* Ph.D. Newcastle: University of Newcastle.

Sylvester, D., 1994. 'Change and continuity in history teaching, 1900-93'. In H. Bourdillon (ed). *Teaching history.* London: Routledge.

The Historical Association, 2001. Teaching the Holocaust. *Teaching History,* 104. London.

The Historical Association, 2007a. Sense and sensitivity. *Teaching History,* 127. London.

The Historical Association, 2007b. Teaching emotive and controversial history 3-19 [online]. Available at http://www.history.org.uk/resources/primary_guide_780_53.html [Accessed 27 March 2009].

Tosh, J., 2008. *Why history matters.* Basingstoke: Palgrave Macmillan.

Wilson, F., 2009. *Two year Key Stage Threes* [online]. Available at: http://www.history.org.uk/resources/secondary_resource_2069_59.html [Accessed 3 July 2009].

With support from:

The Holocaust Education Development Programme (HEDP) is part of the Institute of Education (IOE), University of London and jointly funded by the Pears Foundation and the Department for Children, Schools and Families (DCSF) with support from the Holocaust Educational Trust (HET).